Elijah's Book of Poems (2)

(Keep Knowledge Flowing)

Elijah Latin

Copyright © 2020 Elijah Latin. All Rights Reserved.
No part of this book may be reproduced, stored in a retrieval system, or transmitted by any means, electronic, mechanical, photocopying, recording, or otherwise, without written permission from the author.

Table of contents pg.---(3)

Dedication pg.------------(4)

Acknowledgement pg.--(5)

Introduction pg.----------(6)

(Poems)
Chapter 1 pg.---(7)
Spiritual & Inspirational

Chapter 2 pg.-- (55)
Love

People pg.--------(92)

Chapter 3 pg.----(101)
Humor

War pg.---------- (147)

Drugs pg.--------(150)

Author's short Story (153)

Korhville Poem-pg.-------------(197)

Favorite Eating Spots- pg.-(199-200)

Pastor Inspired Poems-pg.-(202/203)

3

Dedications

I dedicate this book to my family, friends, and to my special friends from the country, my Korhvillians, Tomballers, Hufsmithers, and to the 5 oldest women and next in line pioneers of Korhville Texas. Aunt Nellie Curtis, Mrs. Vollie Franklin, Mrs. Irene Mosley, Mrs. Billie Stewart, Sister Marylou Carter and Mrs. Ruby Miller. Next in line, Dorothy Blanton, Annie Whitfield, Annie Woods, Geraldine Edwards, Juanita Simpson, Lela Kaye Hunt, Katherine (Cat), Brenda Curtis, Delores Cossey, Joyce Cossey, Maxine Lott, Ernestine Godfrey, Barbara Woods, Barbara Brown, Joyce Battles, Joyce Wallace, Helen M., Claire Nell, Lillian Ruth, Gwen, Rosie W., Mary W., Joann, Erlene Solomon, and to the oldest men pioneers. Albert Stewart, his brothers, Freddie, Nolan and Sam, O'Neal Woods Jr., Leon Woods, Joe Whitfield, Freddie L. Solomon, James Solomon, David Solomon, Mr. Horace C. Stewart, Wilford Cossey, Anthony Green, James Jeffery, Arthur Curtis, Ronnie Patterson, Freddie Williams, Joe Green, Melvin Williams, Lonnie Green Jr., and Mr. Marion Blakes Jr. who was grafted in through marriage, and became one of the fellas, and to all whom I have met along the way on my life's journey.

If I missed you, it's because you are not that old yet. To the seasoned pioneers of Korhville Texas I dedicate this book.
With Love, Elijah Latin. (Nook)

Acknowledgements

I want to thank God for giving me the inspiration to write this book of poems and all that He has done and is doing for me.
God is Good all the time.
I want to thank my wife Debra and my sons Wesley and Major for their love and support and all their help with this project while on this great and wonderful journey. It is a joy and blessing for me.
I want to thank my sisters and all my family for their help and all their support.
I want to thank in their memory, my mother in-law and father in-law, Mr. Mcloy and Martha Medlock for supporting me.
I want to also thank in memory of my mother, Mrs. Mable Sias Latin, for my strict upbringing in a strong Christian home.
I want to thank all my Church family, my Pastors, and their wives for their support.
I also want to thank the staff at Amazon KDP publishing for all their hard work in making it possible for me to publish my book and reach people abroad and local, hassle free.
Thanks, Amazon, for all that you do.
I want to thank each of you for your support and friendship.
A special shout out and thanks to all my friends in Korhville Texas, and Hufsmith. The place to be, the country.
All the Glory goes to God, Amen, Jesus is Lord.
Thanks again everyone.

Introduction

It is good when a person can write about things and become that being, that thing or that person whom he or she is writing about. I believe that we all have some form of a poem inside of us. We are inspired to speak out with words on paper or verbally, that others might enjoy what we have stored up on the inside, releasing deep feelings and vast imaginations of the mind and inspirations of the heart.

Some of what we have is Spiritual and inspirational, while love being the key to all that flows within and without. There is the humorous side that helps bring some laughter to a sad countenance and help to maintain a connection to subjects and the general audience.

We speak for the trees, the animals, we speak for beings and things alike. We put ourselves in our subject's stead. Throughout the book I speak for inanimate things and some things are from my life's self-experiences and journeys.

The book is full of joyful, inspirational, spiritual, love, and humorous poems. I have also added a short story of my life growing up in the country, in a little place north of Houston Texas, called Korhville Texas, and I have included a few of my favorite eating places. This book was written with lots of love, inspirations of the heart, and great imaginations. Enjoy.

Chapter (1)

Spiritual/Inspirational

My Sheep Know My Voice

Saints who are following Jesus know His voice,
They will make no other choice.

If one strays from the flock, Jesus will forgive him,
He will not forsake them.

If he repents of his sins, be true, humble, and bold,
He'll be accepted back into the fold.

Jesus is the good Shepherd Who watches over the flock,
He's on duty around the clock.

Having a voice of Authority that one cannot confuse,
His flock He will never abuse.

For His flock, the Shepherd has a very great love,
Because it comes from God above.

There was a loyal sheep who prayed and shed tears,
The Lord added to his life more years.

Whenever the Lord calls and His voice you do hear,
Do not be afraid, go and draw near.

Friendship Of A Saint

I had to write this poem about you,
It was the least I could do.

You have shown me the light, being my teacher,
I often think of being a preacher.

All the mistakes that I could not see,
You've shown them to me.

For what you have done I am so grateful,
Filled with love I'm not hateful.

From the signs it's not hard to tell,
You treat people very well.

To many you are a good friend indeed,
Helping a stranger in need.

You know that I can only say so much,
Your kindness has a magic touch.

Because of you I'm writing much better,
Next time I'll send a letter.

Do not mind me if I don't talk a lot,
Seems like ignoring but it's not.

Most people know that I'm a little shy,
It's time for me to say good-bye.

Upon This Rock

Jesus did say, upon this Rock I will build my Church,
We should view our bodies as such.

According to the Holy scriptures, Peter was a Rock,
Being a Christian is around the clock.

The Church of the Lord Jesus Christ is in you,
The Holy spirit lives there too.

The building is a House of Prayer, Worship and teaching,
It wasn't built for false preaching.

Are you the Church that's built on sand that will wash away?
Or the Rock that's here to stay?

The Rock of the Lord Jesus Christ can stand the test of time,
Build on it while in your prime.

Know that your body is the temple of the Holy Ghost,
Of yourself you will not boast.

Being chosen by Jesus as a Rock for God's glory,
Never tire of telling His story.

When Jesus Stops By

Jesus stopped by Peter's house and sickness had to leave,
To Christ we should always cleave.

Jesus passing by caused a lame man to get up and walk,
Jesus could heal just by His talk.

Jesus rested at a well and a woman called the village men,
She told them of Jesus who knew about her sin.

A girl died and when Jesus arrived death couldn't stay,
The people longed for Jesus to pass their way.

A woman heard how Jesus was healing around the globe,
She was healed just by touching His robe.

Jesus went to Lazarus's grave and raised him from the dead,
Thanking the Father as He lifted His head.

A man cried, Thou Son of David and would not let Him be,
Jesus's touch made him able to see.

Jesus caused a man with palsy to walk and take up his bed,
If not for Jesus, we'd all be dead.

Book Of Instructions

God gave us a Book of instruction and rules to read,
To the Word we should take heed.

If it's a long and prosperous life we want to live,
To God Praise and Glory, we must give.

The Book teaches us about the ways that we should serve,
We shouldn't get on our mate's nerve.

It teaches us that man cannot live on bread alone,
The Word is marrow to the bone.

We learn that Jesus came so that we may have life,
A man finds a good thing in a wife.

The Book tells us that with our son we should not fight,
When we chasten, do it right.

To read and hear the Word you do not have to be a scholar,
Grace and Mercy doesn't cost a dollar.

Out of the Book get wisdom, knowledge and understanding,
Doing the things that God's commanding.

Why Do You Go To Church?

Do you go to Church to see who is who, or just to see who will be the best dressed on Sunday, and can't wait until you get to work and gossip about them on Monday?
Why do you go to Church?

Do you go to learn of Jesus by hearing the Word from God's chosen Preacher, or do you go to be with the crowd, sitting warming the bench and not listening to the teacher?
Why do you go to Church?

Do you go that you may hear and receive the Word of God, and grow in Christ and become a new creature, where old things are passed, and your life takes on a new feature?
Why do you go to Church?

Do you go that you may assemble yourselves and dwell with the brethren, so that in this smoked filled world of sin, you and your house will have God's covering.?
Why do you go to Church?

Do you go that you may serve God, Praise, Worship and give Him the Glory and not just look for an opening or opportunity to tell your own story?
Why do you go to Church?

When God Cleans You

God said, what I have cleaned, let no man call unclean,
He doesn't do it just to be seen.

When we try to clean ourselves, we leave a lot of dirt,
Causing ourselves a lot of grief and hurt.

We overlook the huge plank that's in our own eye,
While seeking a piece of the earthly pie.

Because of being filthy and unclean like an oily rag,
About little petty things we often nag.

We run around being self-righteous and bold,
While our hearts are unclean and cold.

You refuse to take a drink from the Lord's cup,
With Him you will not sup.

If you are running around being rowdy and flirty,
Your mind and heart are still dirty.

If you think that you cleaned yourself, you missed a spot,
Check yourself and see what you got.

Jesus is the only way that you can be cleaned and saved,
A straight and narrow road He has paved.

A cleaning by the Lord will put you on the World stage,
Your life will have a brand-new page.

Changing your ways and true cleaning calls for a fast,
Only what's cleaned by God will last.

Elijah And Elisha

Elijah was a chosen prophet of the almighty God,
He did things that for man were hard.

Elijah prayed that Heaven would withhold her rain,
His praying was not in vain.

Going down to and living by a little brook,
His feats are written in the Book.

To hide from king Ahab there were not many havens,
At the brook he was fed by ravens.

While sleeping under a tree an Angel cooked him two meals,
Elijah had a long journey and no wheels.

In the land of famine, a widow woman was sorely stressed,
But for her obedience she was richly blessed.

Elijah had an apprentice, Elisha, with whom he walked,
Elisha gained knowledge as they talked.

Elijah let the king know that his soul was not for hire,
He was taken up to Heaven in a Chariot of fire.

Elisha saw him being taken and his fate was set in motion,
Filling Elijah's shoes were more than a notion.

In the corner of a house a man and wife made him a bed,
Elisha gave life back to their son who was dead.

When You Know

As a child you are taught about the right and wrong way,
Their paths will cross yours each day.

Parents are to teach their children the way they should go,
This is a must for a child to know.

The Bible says the fear of God is the beginning of knowledge,
This a child should know without going to college.

Things of today are very sophisticated and demanding,
Strive to get wisdom and understanding.

Make sure that you know, who is who, and two plus two,
Be prayerful and observant in all you do.

If you don't want your happiness to be defeated,
Do unto others how you want to be treated.

If it's with the Lord Jesus Christ who you are walking,
Your Holy lifestyle will do the talking.

When encountering a person who always brags,
You'll see the signs and red flags.

Having Faith

Most people don't test their faith thinking they may fail,
Giving the gossipers a story to tell.

When you have faith even the size of a mustard seed,
You can do a humanly impossible deed.

The disciples of Jesus knew and used what they had,
The Holy Ghost wasn't just a fad.

People were healed from the shadow of Peter passing by,
Faith will dry the weeping eye.

On an island Paul was bitten by a venomous snake,
He shook it off like a piece of cake.

Elijah's faith enabled him to part the Jordan river,
In all his tasks he did deliver.

With their faith, Peter and John caused a lame man to walk,
They did more than just talk.

Across the land with faith the disciples cast out the devil,
Their power came from a higher level.

I Will Not Mumble Nor Grumble

Because the Lord wakes me and keeps me in my right mind, I will not mumble.
He feeds me when I am hungry, gives me water when I am thirsty, I will not grumble.

Because Jesus is my Rock, my salvation, my deliverer, and my peace- keeper, I will not mumble.
Though I might be mistreated by some, Jesus sends me a friend to talk with, I will not mumble.

Although I do not have a big bank account, my bills are behind, my phone doesn't work, I will not grumble.
My house is not a mansion, my roof may leak, my grass needs mowing and my gate don't close, I will not mumble.

Even though they talk about me, criticize me, tear me down, never giving me a helping hand, I will not grumble.
When family turn on me, turn me away, knock me down, step on me and stab me in the back, I will not mumble.

My car may be raggedy, need tires, smoking and may not pass inspection, I will not grumble.
Because I have a savoir in Christ and can do all things through Him who strengthens me.
I will not, Mumble nor Grumble.

But Come Sunday

Will somebody please tell me, why is it that every day, Monday through Friday, and some Saturdays, you can get up before the crack of dawn, and it's hard to see your way,
But come Sunday.

Sunday night you set your alarm clock, or device to wake you up bright and early Monday morning, jumping out of bed so you will not be late for work, rushing to join the early flock,
But come Sunday.

Tuesday morning before the rooster crow your eyes are opened and your feet are already hitting the floor, an hour later you are ready to go, by-passing breakfast,
But come Sunday.

Wednesday before the sun rise, you're up and raring to go, wiping the sleep from your eyes, filling a bag with your favorite snack, taping a show to watch when you get back,
But come Sunday.

Thursday before the clock can alarm you are already out of bed and running the comb through your head,
But come Sunday.

When Friday morning, payday rolls around you don't miss a beat, thinking of ways to spend your money, and before the sun comes up you are on your feet,
But come Sunday.

Most of the time for some people on Saturday mornings they are off and have an option, get up or sleep late, laying there with no thoughts of their fate,
But come Sunday.

Sunday morning it's time for church, no alarm clock, no rising early, no wiping sleep from your eyes, no rooster crowing, no payday, it's a day of Worship and Praise.
The devil messes with your head, keeping you in bed,
putting you in a daze,
But come Sunday.

If you can get up early every morning but Sunday, the devil has you on his hook, he doesn't want you to assemble and hear the Word from the Good Book; for he knows God will get the Glory, and all the devil wants is for your life to be just another sad story. Be cheerful, glad and ready to go give God the Glory. Up early every day- **But come Sunday**. Amen.

House Out Of Order

We know a foundation will not stand in a divided house,
There'll be strife with a bickering spouse.

God laid out the solid Rock on which a man should build,
A good home and fruit you will yield.

God's order of doing things, God, man, woman, and child,
Changing God's order things get wild.

Today's parents are letting their children raise themselves,
The Bibles are put away on shelves.

Some Church leaders will place on the people a heavy yoke,
Filling their pockets while hiding behind the cloak.

For a solid foundation, follow the blueprint of the Lord,
But with the crooked and shady cut the cord.

Take those rules and regulations off the shelf and read,
God's instructions we'll always need.

Watch and pray staying inside God's border,
Making sure your house is in order.

Living Your Funeral

You know in this life as the saying go,
You reap what you sow.

When you're growing a garden and you plant beans,
At harvest time don't expect greens.

Just so you know, you can't bake a potato,
And expect a fried green tomato.

If it sings, flies and looks like a mockingbird,
Then it is a fowl, take my word.

Treat your neighbor and fellow man justly and right,
At all cost try to avoid a fight.

For others and all things, don't be envious and greedy,
Always give a helping hand to the needy.

Do not covet, lie, or falsely accuse anyone,
So, of you it'll be said, well done.

The way you live is the way you'll be put away,
You live your funeral every day.

Daily Struggles

For some, getting out of bed each morning is a struggle,
Morning come quickly so you lay and snuggle.

Deciding which shoes to put on, what dress or suit to wear,
Wondering if she or he will be there.

Avoiding the hazards and not being a victim of road rage,
Trying to avoid being locked in a cage.

At the grocery store sifting through the broken carts,
Trying to avoid the devil's darts.

Trying not to be a victim or have anything stolen,
Hoping not to get your lips swollen.

Being disrespected by the young and the old,
Going to work whether it's hot or cold.

Having to raise children in a world full of evil and hate,
Know that God is the author of your fate.

To all who endures to the end and for all that it's worth,
There'll be no struggling on the New Earth.

For What It's Worth

When you wake each morning, give thanks for another day,
Not taking the wide road but the narrow way.

Working for God's Kingdom and doing a good deed,
Shining the light of a loving seed.

Lifting the spirits of strangers, love ones and friends,
Tying together loose and broken ends.

Never failing to make an honest living,
Being able and cheerful in giving.

You can warm a cold heart like melting Jell-O,
Just by saying a simple Hello.

Being neighborly and doing good things because it's right,
Praying for one another day and night.

For a family and all of us to be on one accord is grand,
A house divided cannot stand.

Life only comes around for you one time here on earth,
You must determine for you, what it's worth.

Playing The Harlot

This is another one of those cases where if the shoe fit,
Then you know that must be it.

Now if I were going to be a playboy, I would dress the part,
I would do it with all my heart.

Don't get me wrong, I have not been a Saint all my life,
I changed after settling down with a wife.

There is a dress code in the Bible for Saints that we ignore,
It starts at home, need I say more.

Without going into details or trying to be smart or rude,
Chapter 1:23 in the Book of Jude.

Christians there is a dress code, 1st Timothy two and nine,
This is not just a saying of mine.

Missionaries, ladies, teachers with splits and dresses so tight,
How do you teach others if you're not walking right?

If you have changed and living Holy, you have new cares,
So why are you looking like a harlot showing your wares?

Seasoned Women

The Book of instructions on how we should live,
Instructions to our children we're to give.

Mothers are to teach daughters about the wrongs and rights,
Against evil there'll be plenty of fights.

Seasoned women teach the young how to go and come in,
Teaching them about the wages of sin.

Teach the girls how to act and dress according to Holiness,
For all sins they must confess.

Showing how not to walk as the world if you're a Saint,
How to stay strong and not faint.

Letting her know a married woman should dress the part,
Having wisdom and understanding in her heart.

There are portions of her body only her husband should see,
She should not go around like a busy bee.

The duties of a seasoned woman are in the Good Book,
All you need to do is open it and look.

Moving Forward

The Lord has blessed us to make it through another year,
Enjoying family and friends from far and near.

We should rejoice and be thankful for the good times we had,
Thanking God for bringing us through the bad.

No matter if you were in the mud or wherever you stood,
The Lord worked it out for your good.

The little petty stuff we go through should not be a bother,
We should focus on pleasing the Father.

After you have tried your best and it's all said and done,
You will not please everyone.

Don't take old drama with you into the New Year,
Be encouraged and of good cheer.

Get knowledge and understanding in Bible Schooling,
Give a neighbor a ride by carpooling.

Move into the New Year leaving behind all hate,
Take Jesus with you assuring your fate.

Refrain from being among the backbiter and tail bearer,
Do not become a message carrier.

Seek the Lord and strive to reach higher heights,
Avoiding verbal and physical fights.

Questions?

Have you ever heard the expression, "they come from a good home"?

What are the ingredients, characteristics or what makes a good home?

Is it the Fancy car? Big house, expensive attire? The elegant meals or eating at expensive, fancy restaurants? Living in a plush gated community and going to the finest schools? Looking and talking down to others less fortunate than you?

Thinking that your kids are better than your neighbor's and living faultless?

Eating and talking proper to make yourself look good in front of others and having the best or that dream job? Going to Church every Sunday just to make a showing? Smiling with a hidden frown? Being a person of authority, giving favors with strings attached.

Love is the key and main ingredient. Why **Love**? because **God** is **Love**, without **Love** you are nothing and have nothing. **Love** mends the broken heart, **Love** sets the captive free, **Love** looks beyond the fault and see the need. **Love** will pick you up when you fall, feed you when you hungry and give you water when you thirst, thirst after righteousness.

Love will not boast of itself or falsely accuse its neighbor. **Love** your wife, your husband, your kids and **Love** your neighbor as yourself. **Love** is unconditional and not prejudice, **Love** will hide a multitude of sin, **Love** will forgive and forget. **Love** makes a good home.

Love died for you and me so that we may have life and have it more abundantly. For **God** so **Loved** the world.

Forgiving And Forgetting.

It's often said and heard, I can forgive but I can't forget,
Maybe by Jesus you've not been touched yet.

Jesus forgave us and died for us while we were yet in sin,
He opened His heart and let us in.

Even the Lord's prayer teaches us that we must forgive,
If it's Holy that we are trying to live.

The Bible tells us that God forgives and forgets,
Some haven't reached that point yet.

Jesus does not keep throwing your past up in your face,
He elevates you to a better place.

Man will say forget it, but he never really lets it be,
It shows and comes out for all to see.

What does, not forgetting about it do for your heart?
It keeps friends and love ones apart.

Forgiving helps us get through the stormy weather,
Forgiving and forgetting works together.

Walking With Paul

The day that the Lord called the chief of sinners, Paul,
By Christians he was the most feared of all.

On the road to Damascus the Lord appeared in a great Light,
After that day Paul had a different fight.

After hearing from Jesus, Paul was blind for three days,
He had to suffer for Jesus and change his ways.

After receiving the Word and power of the Holy Ghost,
Of himself Paul did not boast.

Paul learned that walking with the Lord there was a cost,
The old things and ways must be lost.

Being a missionary Paul had to traveled abroad,
Nothing for God was too hard.

Paul sailing on a sinking ship, but not a soul was lost,
Paul preached the Gospel knowing the cost.

Apostle Paul was not ashamed of his walk and preaching,
Paul died dedicated to the Lord's teaching.

Oh, Ye Of Little Faith

In the world today we see more and more Preachers, Pastors, and Bishops, Missionaries and Evangelist failing the Church, while smiling and looking through barred windows from a safe high perch.
Faith?

Preaching their own form of Christianity, twisting the Word of God, turning the truth into a lie, prosperity is their main theme and goal, for the little people making it hard.
Faith?

Preaching and teaching one thing and boldly doing another, walking in darkness and hiding from the marvelous light, never really caring about or loving their brother and doing that which is right.
Faith?

Walking around strutting like a rooster while looking like a pimp daddy and a one-eyed cat, flattering the women and making young men envious, while making their pockets fat.
Faith?

Being tossed around with every little mishap or wind that blow, in them the spirit of truth and love rarely has a chance to flow.
Faith?

Jesus is not the Author of confusion, stealing, murder, lying, mayhem and lasciviousness, or riotous living, He is the giver of life and joy, a saver, a burden bearer and He just keeps on giving. Oh, ye of little Faith?

Just Saying

We read about the female prostitute, what about the male?
He too puts his body up for sale.

With shady preachers the buildings are beginning to fill up,
They drink from the devil's cup.

Preaching and reaching for the money and being greedy,
Depriving the widows and the needy.

Flying in a jet, riding in a Mercedes bragging and boasting,
Setting their souls up for a hot roasting.

Unwilling to share with family or neighbors and never giving,
While a sinful life they're living.

The Bible has guidelines for us all, especially for men of God,
The instructions are simple and not hard.

A Bishop to be blameless, a deacon not taken to much wine,
It doesn't say you can't drink from the vine.

Get in a Church home where the Gospel is being preached,
Where people and souls are being reached. "Just saying."

Throwing A rock And Hiding Your Hand

We all know somebody who likes to point fingers,
If I'm lying, yellow jackets have no stingers.

They'll tell a lie quicker than they can open their mouth,
Then duck and dodge running south.

Telling secrets that was given to them by a friend,
Spreading lies that'll never end.

Stealing from family and neighbors then saying you did not,
Everybody knows you do that a lot.

When getting ready for any function you are always late,
Causing people having to wait.

You're always spying on and accusing your neighbor,
You too cheap to pay for good labor.

You do things that you know are not right,
Then be the first to start a fight.

Ashamed to show your face, you bury your head in the sand,
Always throwing a rock and hiding your hand.

What Can Jesus Say About You?

Can Jesus say, "Well done, my good and faithful son,
A good race you have run?"

Depart from me worker of iniquity, I know you not?
Now into the lake where it's seven times hot.

You did not visit me when I was sick or in jail,
You sold your soul to the devil in hell.

Follow me and I will make you a fisher of men,
Walking with Me you're sure to win.

Brothers and sisters of God whom I love to bless,
Stay away from confusion and mess.

You stayed strong, endured and you finished the race,
For you I have prepared a better place.

While on earth you obeyed your mother and father,
Your neighbor's wife you didn't bother.

Can Jesus say, "your name is written in the Book of life?
You loved me, the Church and your wife?"

A Good Role Model And Example

Being a man identifying with the Lord making a good bed,
All old things you must shed.

Being great does not make one a good person or being,
A lack of good parenting is what we're seeing.

Being a follower of the Lord and doing God's will,
Obeying the Commandments," Thou shall not kill."

Training up your child in the way they should go,
The Lord is the one who they need to know.

Having a tender heart full of kindness and love,
Being harmless as a dove.

Not being a liar, backbiter, talebearer, or willful sinner,
Pray over your food, breakfast through dinner.

Being famous or driving fancy cars does not make one good,
You can't get diamonds from wood.

Whatever is in a person, good or bad, is what will come out,
Being anchored in Jesus is what life's about.
"Jesus is the one and only Perfect Example and Role Model."

Fair Weather And Crisis Saints

Let us start off with the fair-weather Saints of today,
The ones who the slightest wind can sway.

Oppose authority and disagreement by throwing a punch,
With a hungry stranger, no sharing of lunch.

Sunday in Church jumping, shouting and praising hard,
When a disaster strikes, they curse the Lord.

In the daytime they hide and afraid to come out at night,
The devil say boo! They're the first in flight.

Now the crisis Saints in the time of trouble finds religion,
For scammers they become a target and pigeon.

When things are calm, they live isolated like a pea in a pod,
Disaster hits, they bunch up calling on God.

Merchants prey on customers with those jacked up prices,
They lay in wait for the next crisis.

They speak to one another and call each other friend,
Soon as God has fixed it and the trouble end.

No loving and caring, with Christ, no more participation,
Back to the old ways of hating and separation.

Do You Really Love The Lord?

You walk around every day with your head down,
Greeting people with a frown.

Not wanting to listen to advice never lifting your head,
Walking around looking half dead.

Jesus Christ is not dead He is alive and well,
This you can show and tell.

If you are not showing kindness, love and affection,
You're headed in the wrong direction.

You say you love God whom you have never seen.
While you treat your brothers mean.

Love is not puffed up, selfish and does not hate,
Having a loving heart is first rate.

Do you walk and follow the example sent by the Father?
Who does your lifestyle bother?

Do not be one who is ruthless, bitter and hard,
Be cheerful while serving the Lord.

Being Like Paul

Be like Paul, not ashamed of the Gospel of the Lord,
The Lord's yoke is easy and not hard.

Spread the Word of our Lord and Savior,
Always be on your best behavior.

I was once a drunkard, liar and a chief sinner,
Because of Jesus now I'm a winner.

Walking in the light I want to stay prayed up,
I will drink of the Lord's cup.

They can lie on me, beat me and throw me in jail,
I know the Lord will pay my bail.

Show love and compassion to all whom you meet,
Be careful where you rest your feet.

Go out into the world on fire being apt to teach,
Filled with God's Word to boldly preach.

Get the full armor of God to block darts of the devil,
Strive to reach Apostle Paul's level.

Who Is Your Example?

You grow up watching and idolizing athletes and movie stars,
Flaunting fancy clothes and expensive cars.

Having set them up on a high pedestal that's out of reach,
To your children this you teach.

Most of what they do is just a show and a game,
This road may put you to shame.

To be near them you will spend your last dime,
You may even commit a crime.

How many times have your idol been shamed or busted?
That famous one who you trusted.

There is one who is a Good Shepard and great example,
For all your needs He's more than ample.

Being near Him does not cost you an arm and a leg,
For His attention you don't have to beg.

The greatest example for whom I will jump and holla,
It is Jesus, in whom I trust and follow.

He lifts your burden, gives you rest, and is not cheesy,
Take on His yoke, it is easy.

God Is My Supplier

God is the one and only Author and finisher of my fate,
The devil and sin are what I hate.

The Lord supplies and furnish me with all my needs,
He gave unto me fertile seeds.

In my life God's Grace and Mercy have I been granted,
The seed of righteousness in me is planted.

Old things in me has slowly faded and gone away,
From this path I will not stray.

From a little small dirt to a stunning golden floor,
God has opened me a better door.

His Son Jesus has filled my heart with thanks and praise,
To the Heavens my arms I raise.

To my trees and garden, the Lord sends His rain,
When I am hurting, He eases the pain.

Because I have the Word and love of Jesus down in my heart,
From His ways I will not part.

I Am Not Complaining

When the Lord wakes me up in the mornings and my body aches, and is racked with pain, if I step outside and get caught out in the rain,
I am not complaining.

Though I deserve and need a raise, because I work overtime and I work hard on my job, I will not mope around and sob,
I am not complaining.

While walking alone, if I am beaten, robbed and at my head a gun gets pointed, it could be worse, that's why I thank God that I'm anointed,
I am not complaining.

Though the insects, birds and squirrels get into my garden and have a ball, there is enough vegetables for us all,
I am not complaining.

That good job that I had which was only five miles from my house, thinking that I had a virus just because I had a cough,
I am not complaining.

God brought me through the storms, the valleys and over the hills, through it all, I'm still able to pay my bills,
I am not complaining. Amen!

When Calamity And Wrath Comes

One thing to remember, only what you do for Christ will last,
Everything else will crumble and past.

When we rebel against God there is a price that we pay,
It happened in the Bible and still happening today.

It rains on the just as well as the unjust, Saint or sinner,
But with Christ you're a winner.

When God steps in and chastens, we look to man's invention,
God has a way of getting our undivided attention.

God has a way of bringing us around and down to our knees,
We fill the Heavens with our pleas.

When man gets too big for his britches and he is living large,
God shows man whose really in charge.

Because of being arrogant and disobedience, some will die,
A lot of families will wonder and cry.

The Lord sits high, looks low and watches all from above,
God chastens them whom He love.

2020, The Year Of Plenty

Has anybody noticed how things in 2020 increased?
The good and the bad that Heaven released.

God never cease to amaze me when He is doing His thing,
Like the rainbow and its colorful ring.

I saw in my garden how corn on one stalk produced 4 ears,
Never seen that happen in all my years.

My tomato plants were loaded with fruit and growing tall,
The peppers, grapevines, squash and all.

We do not want to take the bad with the good,
And accept the Lord's way like we should.

There was an increase in pestilence and a great loss of life,
Losing loved ones cut through hearts like a knife.

There was a great rise in layoffs and unemployment,
Gave us more time for family enjoyment.

There were more people praying and turning to the Lord,
Being disobedient life was made hard.

Out of it all my heart and my soul got a renewing,
Only God knows what He is doing.

Man's Duty

Some men think that they have it made and are very clever,
Generations passes but the Word abide forever.

Man is to till the ground, plant, build and earn a living,
Get understanding and be cheerful in giving.

God has shown what is bad for us and what is for our good,
Showed us how to make things from wood.

We are required to be just, love and walk humbly with God,
On the poor we should not be hard.

We should believe on the name of His son Jesus Christ,
For us Jesus payed a high price.

Follow Jesus's commandment that we love one another,
Do not hate your sister or brother.

Love God with all your mind, heart, strength and not faint,
Jesus blood we must not taint.

Man's duty, fear God, keep His commandments and live,
To those who endure, eternal life He will give.

Jesus said for us to keep watch and to always pray,
He'll be back for the righteous one day.

When You Think No One Sees You

When you do something thinking that you are real keen,
Although you did it in the dark you were seen.

There is one up above who knows all your thoughts,
He sees your every move and your faults.

God knows what you are going to do even before you do it,
When you tell your sidekick let's get to it.

When you are on that high horse that you ride.
From the Lord you can't hide.

Even though you only stole just one little brown penny,
From God, hiding places there aren't any.

Whenever you are in a bad mood and being mean,
All your actions and facials are seen.

You do things in the dark that are hidden in the night,
Day will bring your bad deeds to light.

Instead of evil or acting with hate, spread some love,
Remember, God is watching from above.

Prayer

Know that the prayers of the righteous will avail much,
The hem of Jesus's robe she did touch.

Strive to live peaceable with all men and love your brother,
Continuing in prayer one for another.

No matter what country or state you live in be a Saint,
Men should always pray and not faint.

Watch and pray that you enter not into temptations,
The Bible is fulfilling the Book of Revelations.

When you pray, pray the "Our Father prayer",
In it you will find Jesus is there.

Be counted worthy, escape these things that shall come,
Do not get caught sleeping like some.

Continue in prayer, watching in the same with thanksgiving,
Make sure it's a Holy life that you're living.

It does not matter whether it is night or day,
Man should always pray.

Traveling Down A One-Way Street

Streets are made to go in certain directions and depending on the way you are headed; you may have to make a few corrections.
Just thought I would mention, it may be beneficial for you to pay close attention.

There is a road that leads to death and destruction, it is never finished but is always under heavy construction.
Watch where you are going, be sure the seed is good that you are sowing.

It may look, enticing, promising and good but it's not, at the end of the wrong road it gets hot.
Remember, do not be dismayed or easily swayed.

It is not easy to back down a one-way street, other lost souls following you are sure to meet.
Before entering a dead end, turn around, and make sure you are traveling on solid ground.

There is one who can turn you around from any situation or street, for Him there is nothing that He cannot defeat.
Jesus can turn you around on a dime and give you change, seek Him and stay in His range.
The one and only way to travel, one way to Heaven, and it's not on a road of gravel. The straight and narrow way.

God Just Keeps On Giving

Although we do not deserve the love that Jesus give,
It's because of Him we live.

God gave a man the ability to make a witty invention,
For us to live Holy and fruitful is His intention.

He continues to bless us every day and every year,
He calms us in a time of fear.

He gives us the ability to create a sports arena or dome,
God gave us earth as a temporary home.

He gives us family, neighbors and good friends,
God allows us to travel and rest at Inns.

Even in our disobedience and rebellion He gives us His love,
He keeps watch over us from above.

With our lust and sinful ways, we must get on God's nerve,
Oh, but what an awesome God we serve.

Although some of us, a righteous life we are not living,
Because of His love, God just keeps on giving.

A Supposed To Be Saint Walking With Jesus

Come with me my son, let us take a walk, show me around,
I want to stroll down your old stomping ground.
Let us walk with a smile not a frown.

Okay Lord, the house where I used to stay is gone,
My mother is in a home all alone.
But son, don't you have a house, car and a phone?

That guy there is a drug addict, he used to be my brother.
After he got on drugs, we stopped loving one another.
Don't you both have the same mother?

That girl there is my sister, but now she makes my eyes sore,
I don't claim her as my kin anymore.
Let Me see, what were you before?

Now son, I pulled you out and reshaped you from the miry clay, turned you around and put you on a solid rock to stay.
On my people, your people, are you turning your back and walking away?

Your brother and sister I do not condemn, I still love them,
Are loving and caring just a whim?
No, my son, Love, Grace, Mercy, Compassion and Charity is My Father's way, and My Father's way, is My way. Repent, go and sin no more. Amen.

When You Are High On Jesus

When you have the Word and Jesus hidden in your heart,
In your walk it shows from the start.

You walk around showing a friendly smile for no reason,
You are joyful in and out of season.

Sometimes at work, for no reason you may start to cry,
Co-workers wondering, not knowing why.

While exploring and traveling across the earth's vast land,
You are happy lending a hand.

For the homeless and needed you will take up their plight,
With loved ones you will not fight.

You will never blame God for your misfortune or loss,
You will never cheat your boss.

No matter what life may throw at you or deliver,
Always be a cheerful giver.

Stay high on Jesus and you shall always flourish,
It's His Holy Word you should nourish.

Do Not Be Fooled By The Cup

Thank the Lord for being able to showcase your talent,
And thank Him for being strong and gallant.

There are some who look at a cup's clean outside,
Not seeing in where dirt may hide.

Always leaping, fumbling and running around in a hurry,
What's inside should cause you worry.

We all have seen, or we have had a dirty cup,
Look inside before you take sup.

Some people like to make their cup look clean,
While germs hide inside unseen.

A rich man died whose cup looked clean, but he went to hell,
There's a beggar in Heaven with a story to tell.

There was a man who took sop with Jesus our Savior,
He paid the price for his behavior.

Which cup do you drink from, the one that's clean outside,
Or the one that's clean inside?

Like Father, Like Son

The one and only God said, let there be light,
His Son Jesus said, I am the light

Jesus said, you see me you see the Father,
I and my Father are one.

Jesus said, you reject me you reject the Father,
Not My will but my Father's will.

God said, put no other God before me,
Jesus said, you worship what you know not.

God said, be fruitful and multiply,
Jesus said, the harvest is plenty.

God hates the sin that man does,
Jesus said, go and sin no more.

God raised a valley of dry bones,
Jesus said, I am the resurrection.

Jesus said, forgive them for they know not what they do,
Today you shall be with me in Paradise.

In the beginning was the Word, the Word was with God,
And God was the Word.

The Word came down and dwelled among the people,
Jesus said, I am the Truth, the Light and the Way.

God said, this is my Son in whom I am well pleased,
Jesus said, in My Father's house there are many mansions, I
go to prepare a place for you. Like Father, like Son.

The Mirror

Mirror, can you please help me to see myself a little bit clearer?

Mirror, you stand 7 feet tall, but can you catch me if I fall?

Mirror since you are man-made, can I use you for shade?

Mirror, I've come to you in the past, can you give me a shape that will last?

Mirror, I tell you secrets like a friend, will my sorrow ever end?

Mirror, I'm doing the best I can, will you help me find a good man?

Mirror, my name is Grady, can you help me find a loving lady?

Mirror, in this world I'm frightened, can you have my security tightened?

While looking in me the Mirror, remember, God didn't give you the spirit of a fearer.

I'm just a man-made Mirror, but Jesus is the One to Whom you need to get nearer.

Stop wasting your time talking to me the mirror, I'm not the one to help you see clearer.
Call on Jesus who is Lord, for Him nothing's too hard.

The Lord Is Always With Me

I have walked down and travel over the rough roads,
Jesus helped me to carry the heavy loads.

I have been in deep valleys and climbed up high hills,
Jesus was always on time helping pay the bills.

Because it is the Kingdom of Heaven that I seek,
Jesus helps me to turn the other cheek.

The power and love of Jesus I never doubt,
Of His blessings I'm never left out.

My soul is in His hand to protect and keep,
He watches over me when I sleep.

My pastures are green, and my waters are still,
I strive to stay in God's will.

Each day my head is anointed with blessed oil,
The devils plan the Lord will foil.

Though not deserving the Lord is with me everywhere,
In court, jail and the hospital, Jesus is there.

In living Holy and being righteous there is power,
And Jesus is the Man of the hour.

Chapter (2)

Love

My Rose, My Lily, My Violet

She fits my heart perfectly to a tee,
A beautiful bride she came to be.
She is filled with inner and outer beauty,
Loving her is my appointed duty.

To her children she is a kind wonderful mother,
Teaching them to love each other.
She smothers them with love and affection,
Guiding them in the right direction.

With hair shining like the world's finest silver,
Love and kindness, she will always deliver.
The morning Sun rises to see her smiling face,
In my heart she will always have a place.

With an aroma that is forever present in my nose,
She is my beautiful Texas Rose.
Although she is a wife, mother and arrayed like a Lily,
Every now and then we play and get a little silly.

Because of her being the one and only woman by my side,
Whatever I do for her, I do it with pride.
My love, my Lady, you have put my heart on auto pilot,
You are my wonderful and beautiful Violet.

Precious Blue Bird

This little blue bird has the love of many,
She has a heart that gives plenty.

Her kind and caring love touches are warm hearted,
From her loving ways she has never parted.

There are always words of wisdom in her gentle talk,
A straight and narrow path she does walk.

Her warm and gentle wings of protection,
Covers us with love and affection.

All her days are peaceful and not stressed,
To know her, we are blessed.

To whom shall your love and kindness be compared?
We can see how much you've cared.

Your love showers and cover us like triple rainbows,
From the depts of your heart, love flows.

Thanks for all the wonderful things you have did,
The love you share can't be hid
Fly little blue bird, fly.

Equally Yoked

One cannot pull left and the other pull right,
If so, you're headed for a fight.

Each must be level and pull the same way,
Even when you're having a bad day.

One is not better or above the other,
You must love one another.

Each must help one another with the housework,
Neither should lag or be a jerk.

They both should agree when punishing a kid,
Not disagree and blow a lid.

Both must pull the same way, or you will get nowhere,
In that same spot tomorrow, you'll still be there.

Being equally yoked yields much and is a good thing,
Much blessing does it bring.

One pulling forward, the other pulling backwards is no joke,
Make sure you are wearing an even yoke.

What Will Love Do?

Love will conquer and hide a multitude of sin,
Love will open and let you in.

Love will stand beside you and share the pain,
Love will even share its gain.

Love will teach you right from wrong,
Love will make a weak man strong.

Love will take you places a wise man dare,
Love will show how much you care.

Love will make one not want to believe or see,
Love will let a matter be.

Love will cause one's heart much trouble,
Love will have you seeing double.

Love will turn a wayward child around,
Love will pick you up off the ground

Love will not angrily raise its voice,
Love will give you a choice.

Love will be in the interest of your well-being,
Love will explain what you're seeing.

Love will walk, bend and stretch for miles,
Love will turn frowns into smiles.

Sharing The Overflow

When God blesses us, we are to be a blessing to someone,
Instead we don't want to give away none.

Even when it comes to tithing and giving to the Church,
You hesitate and won't give much.

Where is the love that our Lord and savior shared?
He died for us because he cared.

In a world full of evil, love is the best thing going,
Open your heart and let love make a showing.

We should all make love and charity one of our task,
The Bible says give to everyone that ask.

You pass by a homeless person with your windows rolled up,
Refusing to put a penny in their cup.

You walk around with gold and designer shoes on your feet,
Doing everything but help a hungry person eat.

Open your heart, and spread your wings like a dove,
Showering the needy with blessings and love.

Anybody Can Say I love You

The question is, do you mean it when you say it?
Maybe you just saying it to fit?

Something that we should know, love is an action word,
It's not given just to be heard.

Love is given without any hidden agenda or attaching string,
Loving unconditionally is a wonderful thing.

Love will cause you to help when you do not want to,
Love can make a fool out of you.

There was an old song that said, I am a fool for love,
Love was given from God above.

Love was not given to be discarded or put on a shelf,
Love your neighbor as yourself.

True love will mend the bruised and broken hearted,
Love mourns the dearly departed.

Love will conquer, do a work and a good deed,
Love will help those in need.

A Man Who Finds A Wife, Finds A Good Thing

A woman who is virtuous, considerate, loving and caring,
Her goods she will not mind sharing.

She will raise her children up in the way they should go,
The Lord she will teach them to know.

Away from home and into the darkness she will not stray,
She will rule her house God's way.

She will not be flattered by a man with a smooth word,
In her home her voice will be heard.

To her husband she will be a loving wife of understanding,
Not one who is always demanding.

She will raise up her children and care for her house well,
She will not be carried away by a fairy tale.

She is a woman of good standing, courage and virtue,
With a kind heart she will nurture.

She will not join in with nor tarry long with the sinner,
To her husband she is a winner.

A Beautiful Woman

She is one who always draws attention when she walks,
When men gather, she's the topic of their talks.

When she passes by even the flowers bend and bow,
The honeybee flies by buzzing, wow!

Her beautiful hair waves and flows freely with the wind,
To her beauty there's no end.

Whether it be night or morning she has an everlasting glow,
Each day her beauty continues to flow.

She is a sweetheart that is more precious than gold,
Her heart is never rude or cold.

She is more than a man can ask for during his earthly life,
A man will jump hurdles to make her his wife.

He shows her off, steps out like a king every chance he gets,
Of her beauty there are no frets.

Loving, kindness, tenderhearted and caring tells her story,
Being blessed with beauty is her glory.

A Dear Jane

Now here we go again, it is such a difficult and sad thing,
Asking her to give back the ring.

He does not know the impact of what he is doing,
All night she'll be boohooing.

In her heart she knows that he has left and is gone,
Sweet memories will not leave her alone.

Memories of their wonderful and lovely nights on a date,
Defying her father and bringing her home late.

Her heart and lips longing for just one more kiss,
His loving arms she will miss.

We cannot count the times a heart takes a fall,
It may happen to us all.

Had she not been running around with Pat and Cind,
She would still have her boyfriend.

She found out that hanging with Cind and Pat,
Is not where her heart was at.

Hearing her favorite love song cannot bring her to her feet,
She refuses to let her heart dance to the beat.

Knowing if she does not rise, it will not get any better,
She angrily tears up, the "Dear Jane" letter.

My Wife, Side-Chick And Girlfriend

When you are in love and put on that wedding ring,
As part of your life, that's a good thing.

You travel by sea and by land to seek a wonderful wife,
One that you're dedicated to for life.

A woman who will return the love you so freely give,
One whose love last long as you live.

The one woman who makes your heart skip a beat,
The greatest woman you could ever meet.

The wonderful mother of your children causing no strife
This is your one and only, loving wife.

A woman who will stick by you through thin and thick,
She's your do or die side-chick.

A woman who loves and stays with you until the end,
She is all in one, a Wife, Side Chick and Girlfriend.

You cannot ask for a better wife, friend and woman,
You both having all things common.

My friend and side chick, you are a wonderful wife,
We're one and soul mates for life.

Love Is No Plaything

When your body and your heart desires a mate,
Let God's hand control your fate.

Be careful of the lifetime woman that you choose,
Because it's your heart that will lose.

Do not take chances with your heart and I mean none,
Be sure before the choosing is done.

Take your time before you commit and say I do,
Make sure she loves you too.

You should not have to ask her where she has been,
Before the sun set, she is already in.

A woman like her is a rare thing, you know what I mean.
Find her and make her your Queen.

When you need your woman, she has your back,
In giving love she's not slack.

From above, in your heart the seed has already been planted,
Never take one's love for granted.

Hearts can't be quickly stitched back like a piece of leather,
It takes time to put a broken heart back together.

A Good Man

He is God fearing and one who is kind and humble,
Against work he doesn't grumble.

He knows that a woman must be treated with respect,
Her love he will not reject.

He will love and cherish her all the days of his life,
Being happy that she's his wife.

He will rub her aching body, this is what he prefers,
Letting her know that he's all hers.

He works to supply his home and paying every bill,
A garden for her, he will plant and till.

He will not have roving eyes or wondering hands,
He'll meet all her demands.

To one woman he will commit to and love,
They stay together like the dove.

A good man will stay home, to go astray he will not,
In a good woman he knows what he's got.

He will Worship and do the Lord's will,
All his duties he does fulfill.

Nutrients Of Love

Being caring and kind to a lonely traveling stranger,
Demonstrated by the babe born in a manger.

Sharing increase, blessing and goods with the needy,
For money, never being greedy.

Lifting one up who has taken a fall,
Being eager to answer the call.

Love will keep a secret and never tell,
Love is not for rent or sale.

Love look beyond the faults and see the need,
Love sows a loving seed.

To be in line with the good Book in all clarity,
Where love is you will find charity.

Love is caring, kind, forgiving, gentle and sweet,
Loving your enemy is a great feat.

Love will carve its name in the tree,
Love will set the captives free.

No matter what you have seen or heard,
Love is more than just a word.

Angry, But Sin Not

I know it is always easier said than done, right?
Especially when it comes to a fight.

Some people are prone to loving a person traditionally,
Instead you need to love unconditionally.

People make you angry when they try to be slick,
Upside their head you want to throw a lick.

Stop before you do, take a deep breath and think,
To their level you must not sink.

Being wise, tenderhearted and your patience must be strong,
Jesus is the key to keep you from doing wrong.

Love will see a wrong and try to make it right,
Love will keep you home at night.

Love will keep you from hurting your child,
Love will keep you from acting wild.

With the love of God in your heart, be angry and sin not,
Is this the kind of love that you got?

When one causes your temper to rise, count to ten,
Against evil thoughts you can win.

Seeing Through The Smoke

You venture out into the night visiting the uptown bar,
Your eyes catch the glimpse of a lady in a car.

You were captivated the minute she walked in the door,
She blew your mind just walking across the floor.

Being in a hurry to meet her, you sent over a drink,
Never once did you slow down to think.

Your heart racing, it was beating faster by the minute,
Her heart, you were determined to win it.

Failing to see through all the gloss and make up she wore,
Pausing for a second you would have seen more.

All the men at the bar seemed to know her nickname,
Look like you were late in the game.

Once she pulled off the wig, nails and that tight girdle,
You regret rushing to jump the hurdle.

When at a bar, take it slow while sifting through the smoke,
What you see when it clears may cause you to choke.

Make sure that when you leave you have a clear head,
You may wake up with bridezilla in your bed.

Back In The Day

I can only speak about the time when I was growing up,
When we drank from a well out the same cup.

The elderly, women and girls were all treated with respect,
Going to Church we couldn't reject.

We respected the Lord's house and all the Preachers,
At school we behaved and obeyed the teachers.

Between school and homework, we did all our chores,
We walked to the Mom and Pop stores.

For certain ailments we used milk from a fig,
In elementary school I owned a pig.

We ate fresh vegetables and my favorite was corn on the cob,
During our teenage years we all had a job.

In Korhville there were no robbing and killing one another,
We treated everyone like a brother.

When a person fell, we extended our hand,
We even helped to till the land.

I cannot lie and say that it was all good back in the day,
But in Korhville Texas, we did it our way.

Love Will Listen

When one expresses their feeling and pours out their inner self, one will listen and prepare to release a healing.
When one cries because of the hurt and pain that has been inflicted or unknowingly given by a friend or loved one.
They will listen to instructions and work diligently to prepare the damage that is done.

Never meaning to hurt or cause a loved one pain, searching their heart, long pondering, knowing that the trust of the one who has been hurt, sitting and wondering if their trust.
Will they ever regain?

To talk is the beginning of a connection, over talking can ruin and put distance between communicators but the heart and love is bound and will cease talking, and quietly listen. Love will accept correction.

Love doesn't listen with closed ears, sometimes not heard, love listens with the heart, it spreads kindness, tenderness and charity. It is not easily disrupted or easily torn apart or discarded. Love will examine words.

One must discern between what is good, meaningful conversation and what is bad and unproductive talk. From gossip and tales, one will get up and walk, even when the opposition is wrong, doing it for love and peace sake.
Love will listen.

Marriage And Love Undivided

Your eyes met and you fell ever so deeply in love,
You were inseparable like the dove.

As you dated and cruised around the world together,
You withstood all kinds of weather.

Because of all the love and good things your hearts pitched,
You decided to get hitched.

Now that you are together and have made your bed,
There are things that was not said.

The things that you have now are not just yours alone,
Those days are dead and gone.

The nights are over of being out with the girls or boys,
You must get rid of all your toys.

You both need to be of one mind and on one accord,
Where love lives it's not that hard.

With making vows and saying I do, nothing is divided,
Becoming one, by love your heart is guided.

Some people may be selfish, and others may whine,
Nothing is separated or called mine.

An Angel Of Beauty

What yonder do I see, sparkling and glowing from afar,
More gorgeous than the morning star.

Always and forever radiating the most beautiful glow,
When she moves, she puts on a show.

Her silky black hair blowing and waving in the wind,
To her beauty there is no end.

Just seeing and being around her is not enough,
Leaving her presence is ever so tough.

Having a beautiful smile that puts a wise man in a trance,
To be in her presence he'll take a chance.

Now with that said and letting the truth be told,
She's one who is beautiful and bold.

I have loved and my aching heart has also lost,
For her, my heart will pay the cost.

She is the most beautiful woman I have ever seen,
My heart is determined to make her my Queen.

My Dark Handsome Prince (for the ladies)

He is smooth like coco butter and stands six feet four,
My heart skips a beat when he walks through the door.

His hands hold me so tight with a soothing soft touch,
When he's gone my heart misses him much.

Whenever he walks by the trees take a bow,
Men standing in awe wondering how.

When he comes home, he fills my heart with joy,
Never does he treat me like a toy.

Good love and good music, he knows how to mix it,
If anything is broken, he'll fix it.

As the days go by and I look at my wedding ring,
My eyes cry while my heart sing.

It is good to have a man who loves and treat me right,
He holds me gentle while cuddling me tight.

I am so happy I found my dark handsome Prince,
I found love and have been happy since.

Following The Crowd

Here you go again, following old Dave and John,
Your love life going to be one and done.

Running around drinking and playing the field,
Using your buddies for a shield.

Knowing that you have the love of your life,
The one you want for a wife.

Though you are not married she pays notes on your ride,
After work she waits alone outside.

Always late and out of your mouth comes nothing but junk,
Your breath and eyes tell her you're drunk.

Being too heavy to bear, she decides to lighten her load,
She sent you packing down the road.

Now you can play the field and hang out with the crowd,
Instead you're lonely and not so proud.

You thought that you could hang out like Rob,
The difference is, he's got a job.

One Sided

We were made by God and to each other we are help mates,
Remember that when you're out on dates.

All things should be equal in any relationship,
Take this information as a tip.

There is something that we all must realize and see,
It's not just about you or me.

In a relationship each must learn to take and to give,
In a divided relationship it's hard to live.

There should be no hidden secrets in a relationship or union,
Clear the air like you're taking communion.

Whether just friends or the love of a life soul mate,
Honesty will determine your fate.

Do not be led astray or be one who is misguided,
Loving hearts are not easily divided.

You cannot go around thinking you are to always receive,
It's yourself whom you will deceive.

Remember in a marriage there is some give and take,
You can have your cream and your cake.

Trouble In The Camp

You buy your child a toy, no matter if it be for a girl or boy,
Your aim is to bring them joy.

Yep, you are aged and weary, you must watch your step,
You don't have that same pep.

You are no longer a young pup, it is hard to rise and get up,
You can't get coffee from an empty cup.

When people are acting strange, you must move out of range,
Hoping that their hearts will change.

Be careful how you make your bed, by who you are being led,
Make sure it's God's Word that you're being fed.

Home from work it is time to unwind, today was not so kind,
Now it's time to relax your mind.

Up each morning before seven, takes a lunch break at eleven,
You're trying hard to make it to Heaven.

At a game you are booed, say the wrong thing and get sued,
I didn't know people could be so rude.

I love my kids and wife, my heart has been under the knife,
Praying that my name's written in the Book of Life.

Love Covers

For God so loved the world that He gave His only begotten Son so that whosoever believed on Him shall live and have life more abundantly, the Son laid down His life for us sinners and His friends,
Love covers.

As babes, young children, our mother and father cares for us, feed us when we are hungry, kiss our bruises, clothe us, teach us how to walk, how to talk and how to fend for ourselves,
Love covers.

Love is blind, love sees no color, race or creed, love binds together in Holy matrimony, love is humble, love is sweet and kind to all strangers and love ones alike,
Love covers.

Love will feed the hungry, give to the needy, love is not greedy, love will cause the heart to grieve, love will share one's pain, love is not selfish with its gain,
Love covers.

Love will strive for peace, from an argument love will cease, love will look beyond the fault and see the need, for you love will plead, Love forgives, and love will forget,
Love covers.

The Appearance of Sweet

Some of us learn early in life that looks can be deceiving,
You must discern the signals you're receiving.

You buy a piece of jewelry on just a smile and handshake,
At home you find out that it's fake.

The world is full of deceit no matter which way you turn,
Sometimes it's a hard lesson to learn.

You buy a car from a lot because of its good looks,
Later you find out the sellers were crooks.

It's like buying a tv off the side of the road still in the box,
When you get home, there's nothing but rocks.

You take in at face value a nice warm-hearted little kid,
You find out all the bad acting was well hid.

We see or know people who greet with a fake smile,
You can see them coming for a mile.

In being deceitful, selfish and fake, do not take part,
Love your neighbor with a pure heart.

How Is Your Shadow?

You know what they say, another day, another dollar,
If you need me just holler.

Do you mean it when you say I am here for you every day?
Is it just something that you say?

Do your ways and words make people or a love one cry?
Can you help the needy but never try?

Going out your way to help a stranger you do not dare,
If one is lost, you don't care.

Just long as you have yours the heck with the rest,
At being a friend, you failed the test.

You go around talking about friends behind their back,
In raising your children, you're slack.

You are always in the middle of a he said, she said,
Making enough noise to raise the dead.

There is one thing that you need to know,
Your shadow follows wherever you go.

Thank God For A Loving Wife

She is the apple that put the sparkle in my eyes,
Through the rain I see blue skies.

When the days are long and hard, she knows my struggle,
In her bosom she allows me to snuggle.

She is my soul mate, my wife, my lover and my best friend,
Broken things her caring hands will mend.

She does not have a desire to go and hang out with the girls,
She looks so lovely walking around in her curls.

Walking around in her pajamas when she mops,
I love the way she fills out the tops.

She makes me glad while making me feel like a king,
She causes my heart to sing.

She is my woman, she sticks and stand by my side,
She's in for the long ride.

I will never take my woman or her love for granted,
In my heart her love is planted.

When Lying Becomes Easy

Hey, did you see that truck run that stop sign?
No, I didn't, knowing you lying.

Are you one of those who say I do not want to be involved?
Hoping without you the problem is solved.

Was that your child I just saw break a window and run away?
My child has been inside the house all day.

Here comes that old nosey neighbor, I am going to go hide,
Is your mother home? "no" your kid just lied.

Girl I love your hair "she looks a mess,"
She's still my friend, nevertheless.

Hey friend I need to borrow some money,
Man, mine is looking a little funny.

If you play with fire you are sure to get burned,
This some of us haven't learned.

If you are a liar, get right with God before you die,
Because God Himself hates a lie.

Loving, Caring, And Sharing

Loving the Lord with all your strength, soul and heart,
Loving your neighbor is also a part.

Taking care of home, family and doing the best that you can,
Proving and establishing yourself as a man.

Raise a child the way he should go and not spare the rod,
This is sound doctrine given by God.

For a loved one you should show support and be there,
Let them know how much you care.

Showing love with an open ear and open eye,
Always loving not letting it die.

Being kind and tenderhearted reaching out to those in need,
Never broadcast or boast when doing a deed.

In the garden of life, sharing makes a beautiful showing,
When it's the seed of love you are sowing.

Always love and strive to treat your fellow man fair,
Sharing the good fruit that you bear.

Only God Knows

You can lie to me, fool me with trickery, words and deceit,
One day the rug will be pulled from under your feet.

We know what is done in the dark will come to light,
Nothing is hidden from God's sight.

Sunday your money is at home you put nothing in the plate,
Boldly you ask the Lord to bless your fate.

There is one up above who sits high and looks low,
Knows when you are putting on a show.

He sees you when you mistreat your brother,
Even when you're cursing your mother.

When being deceitful, to you it is no bother,
God hears how you talk to your father.

Only God knows what is hidden in one's heart,
He will forgive and grant you a new start.

God knows your pain and sees when you cry,
Your tears the Lord will dry.

The Honey Do

The two most famous words heard at home in a marriage,
The moment you carried her inside from the carriage.

Men hear those words more often after they retire,
For all we do, we should be for hire.

The smart man keeps handy the reliable hurt back card,
Especially when it comes to mowing the yard.

After getting home from work and before you can shower,
She hands you a shovel and says plant this flower.

Saturday on your rest day she comes to you with a broom,
Here you go honey clean the room.

Soon as you finish helping her with the last chore,
She hands you a list to go to the store.

Your love for her allows you to let the honey do slide,
When you hear her coming, you learn to hide.

Get used to it married men and learn to think fast,
The Honey do is made to last.

Where Love Lives

Where love lives, there also peace will be in the home,
Giving a spouse no reason to roam.

Where love lives, there will be happiness and joy,
No need for games or a play toy.

Where love lives, there will be comfort from hurt and pain,
No one will be left standing in the rain.

Where love lives, in stormy weather things will be fine,
Nothing will be marked as mine.

Where love lives, out of the heart flows healing powers,
Money and assets will be called ours.

Where love lives, in the marriage it is not just about me,
Instead of arguing, you'll let it be.

Where love lives, you are real and your love is not fake,
In a relationship there's give and take.

Where love lives, gentleness and caring wipes away tears,
Love gets stronger through the years.

A Letter To All

One day God decided to make a place He called earth,
He formed a man and woman and she gave birth.

As time passed, man tilled the earth and multiplied,
God said man should be sanctified.

To mankind, life brings new, exciting adventure each day,
Man must travel the straight and narrow way.

God sent His son Jesus to save the sinner,
Jesus wants you to be a winner.

Jesus said we should love one another as He have loved us,
Not walk around keeping up a fuss.

God forgives us and forgets it, and let bygones be,
He throws it into the forgetful sea.

When the love of God from above gives your heart a tug,
It's time to give someone a hug.

As much as possible, God wants us to live in peace,
From all bickering we should cease.

Loving The Little Things That She Does

When I said I do, I married her for better or worse,
She's my soul mate and perfect nurse.

She is always there for me and I am never lonely,
Her eyes are for me only.

When she is away her gentle touch I do miss,
She always greets me with a sweet kiss.

In the kitchen she is busy as a bee making sure that I am fed,
Sometimes she feeds me breakfast in bed.

She walks in a way that she knows will catch my eye,
She throws me a kiss when she walks by.

Every time I see her, she makes my heart scream,
She's the only girl of whom I dream.

The way that she touches me and rub my nose,
She warms me from my head to my toes.

Because she is lovely, sweet and kind, I made her my wife,
I promise to love her for the rest of my life.
(Sweet dreams my love)

Running From A Broken Heart

She was waiting for him as he walked through the door,
Telling him that she didn't love him anymore.
With flowers blooming, birds singing and jasmine in the air,
The only place he wanted to be was there.

She had a smile that would set his heart aflame,
It starts skipping at the mention of her name.
She had the beauty of a once in a lifetime queen,
The most beautiful girl he'd ever seen.

Her kisses were sweeter than sweet,
She always swept him off his feet.
The aroma around her gave off a unique smell,
Of its ingredient he couldn't tell.

After saying she did not mean to break his heart,
She said it was best that they part.
Her words flowed through him like a cold chill,
For this ailment, the doctor had no pill.

His broken heart quickly began to race,
As he glanced into her face.
His arms were trying to reach out to her and cleave,
No part of him wanted to leave.

His lips yearned for just one more kiss,
Her sweetness they would miss.
The radio was playing their favorite song,
His heart felt like it was hit with a gong.

She turned from him staring at the blank wall,
The phone rang and she answered the call.
Because of the hurt and his foolish pride,
He decided to run away and hide.

Who Am I?

Though all through life I have caused her much pain and sorrow, she never complains or brings it up.
She is my Landlord and keeper of my house and my secrets, though she charges me not for all that she does.
Though she teaches me right from wrong and guides me towards a path that is straight and narrow, she bends, but never breaks.
While I do not always choose or do the things that are right, she never forsakes me, leaves me hanging or standing out in the rain.
To me she will give and for me she will spend her very last penny, while in her house there is no bread, she gives me comfort. Against me she refuses to receive an accusation and for me she will stand and fight with every breath of her dear life.
Although she may be tired, weary and heart broken, she still smiles while showering me with love and affection.
Though she is my teacher, keeper, and caregiver, she is the best friend one can ever have here on earth, in the flesh.

My love for her goes deeper than what the eye can see and what money can buy, because when the Lord calls her home, another like her, there will never be. I Love You, I Love You, I Love You. Tell her now, show her now. Love lifts, love mends, and love forgives.
So, who am I? I am my mother's wayward child.

People

The Lot Guy

The lot guy is underpaid and overworked,
Everyday his chain is jerked.

Managers are always giving him extra to do,
Sometimes yelling at him too.

Although he often works out in the sun,
Sometimes he has a little fun.

He works hard for just a little bit of pay,
Friendly people help make his day.

An angry customer dumps on him hard,
He does nothing to deserve it Lord.

Co-workers and managers are always using him,
Sometimes he hides from them.

Some day he and this old job will part,
He's looking for a new start.

He can't stop and tell other workers how he feels,
A manager is always on his heels.

A Boxing Great

To be a boxer his body was geared,
Of his punch most men feared.
Becoming the world champion was his thing,
Whenever he stepped in the ring.

Some people sized him up from a glance,
They said he didn't stand a chance.
For the boxing title he had a thirst and hunger,
Facing opponents who were younger.

The master of boxing entered the ring with a plan,
He was knocking out the younger man.
His opponent heard the crowd roar and a loud humming,
It was the future champ coming.

Showing the world that he was the true boss,
He wasn't going to take a loss.
He did something that he had done before,
He knocked his opponent to the floor.

To the chin he connected with a left and right,
His opponent was out like a light.
All around the world it could be heard,
His name became a household word.

Ride-um Cowboy (R.M.) The 44

He was very friendly and smiled all the time,
He was a great cowboy during his prime.
He became a household name in his hometown,
He never let nothing get him down.

He was real and one of the toughest cowboys around,
He had a big smile when he hit the ground.
When riding wild broncs, he showed no fear,
He climbed aboard every year.

On weekends we were ready to see him put on a show,
His name the world would get to know.
We enjoyed the rodeo, but he enjoyed it more,
He became seasoned and hardcore.

He was a laid-back guy, strong willed and easy going,
He always made a good showing.
From Rodeo to everyday life I could not write it all,
I wrote about a few things on his life's wall.

This cowboy was blessed with a gentle soul and kind heart,
Having a love for people that would never part.
Here on earth the Lord gave him freedom to roam,
At the appointed time God called him home.

We had good times and enjoyed him while he was here,
It is okay to feel pain, sorrow, cry and shed a tear.
His leaving has left us with a void, and we are sad,
He is in a better place so cheer up and be glad.

The Lord has sent an Angel down to deliver,
His son's soul back to the giver.

A Couple Of Christians

I met him while he was standing underneath a tree,
A Christian I was coming to be.

He was eating a plate of Barbeque next to his car,
They had traveled from afar.

He was a Preacher and his wife was a Missionary,
From appearances they looked ordinary.

For friends and strangers, they were not out of reach,
A Bible band class, his wife loved to teach.

He never preached about something that he heard,
Only preached from the Word.

Always preaching and showing God's way of love,
Earning himself a place above.

To the sick and the needy they always showed pity,
Living on the eastside of the city.

His wife having the heart of a Church mother,
Both knew how to treat one another.

Sheltered each other in a time of stormy weather,
Always in step and praying together,

Surely their names are written in the Lamb's book of life,
God blessed this man and wife.

Martha

Martha was a kind, loving and wonderful mother,
For her children there was no other.

She was a rare find with a tender loving heart,
That was one thing that set her apart.

Martha treated us each with kindness and love,
Placed in her heart from God above.

She brightened our day with her loving touch,
We all miss her so much.

In Martha's heart we always had a home,
Her castle was like a love filled dome.

She embraced us all with a smile and a hug,
Our hearts felt her gentle tug.

She helped us up whenever we had a fall,
Showing that she cared for us all.

A woman's whose love was true and always the same,
Martha Medlock was her name.

Mcloy

Mcloy was blessed with a wonderful wife,
With her beside him he enjoyed life.

Mcloy raised his family to follow God's Decree,
He was a good and fruitful tree.

Always willing to lend someone a helping hand,
Mcloy prospered while tilling the land.

Took to the road with the kids to camp,
He was the grandchildren's champ.

Enjoying a feast and keeping the family together,
They had a bond stronger than leather.

A man who was wise in his decision making,
Mcloy was real and never faking.

For his children and grandchildren, he was concerned,
He desired that they be well learned.

He often invited us over for a good homecooked meal,
His love and kindness were for real.

The Greatest In-laws

Two of the greatest in-laws west of the Mississippi river.
Never made a promise that they didn't deliver.

Raised their children up in the way they should go,
This is something that I know.

To me they never said a negative or unkind word,
Kindness from them I received and heard.

They lived the simple life of working-class people,
Never putting themselves on a high steeple.

They were never too high they could not be reached,
They always practiced what they preached.

Always welcoming travelers and family with open arms,
They were blessed with amazing charms.

They did not build on sand but on solid ground,
For future generations it will be around.

In-laws with a good understanding is a rare find,
Mcloy and Martha were one of a kind.

Boots

Larry Green's time here on earth was well spent,
For his soul, the Lord has sent.

His earthly father left this world ahead of him,
The Lord has reclaimed them.

Some say not to, but it is alright to be sad and cry,
When you are saying that final goodbye.

Remember when His friend Lazarus had died,
The Bible tells us Jesus cried.

With friends and family Boots love was shared,
He showed us all that he cared.

Whenever you saw him, he was in a friendly mood,
When he cooked, he shared his food.

Boots loved to make us laugh with his funny jokes,
Must have been something in them cokes.

In his young adult life, he had a fast 1964 white Ford,
With that car his life wasn't bored.

One-night Boots and Lump left the police in the dust,
Trying to catch them was a bust.

Do not just sit around moping and being sad,
Think of the good times that you had.

If God open Heaven and show us Larry Green's File,
The first thing we'd see would be a smile.

Chapter (3)

Humor

Trouble Making Right Hand

Okay Righty don't do anything stupid,
Like the time you played cupid.

You offered that little lady a dip,
She busted old Dave's lip.

Remember when I told you not to fight,
I ended up getting cut that night.

Then you looked at that tall man's wife,
He pulled out a carving knife.

Then there was the time at the Rodeo,
I told you that we should go.

On a policeman you spilled two drinks,
He put us both in iron cuff links.

Then that Friday night down at the bar,
You leaned on that big man's car.

He twisted you like a soft piece of metal,
I had to wait for the dust to settle.

I cannot count all the scrapes we've been in,
Starting fights that we couldn't win.

Since I am always pulling your fat out of the fire,
This left hand should be for hire.

They Call Me Money

I was made to be given in exchange for services and goods,
I can be made from trees in the woods.

I was not made to make people sad,
I was made to make them glad.

Although I am known to be evil's main root,
You can't make it without any loot.

I am the cause of many people being sent to jail,
Some put their souls up for sale.

I am argued over in marriage and in divorce,
Some even try taking me by force.

I have never been seen by some far away tribes,
Sometimes I'm given and received in bribes.

It may seem very funny at times, but it's no prank,
Sometimes I am robbed from a bank.

I am money, a source of power and wealth.
My best wishes to man's good health.

That Pesky Mockingbird Again

I don't mind the birds playing around in the yard,
There's one that's always on guard.

I said that if they didn't bother me it would be fine,
Long as they know that the yard's mine.

Trouble begins when the mama flies to the back,
From my garden she likes to snack.

One morning when I opened the bedroom drapes,
There she was eating my grapes.

She keeps watching for the tomatoes to turn red,
Even tried dropping a bird pie on my head.

She walks through the garden like she owns the place,
Pausing to look me in the face.

I went to Lowes and bought me some bird netting,
No more grapes will she be getting.

She got tangled in the net and almost didn't get free,
After that she let my garden be.

The Bold Squirrel

I thought the Mockingbird was the worse pest I had,
But that squirrel is just as bad.

The squirrel is one of the reasons I let the bird be,
She chases the squirrel away for me.

The Mockingbird flies down and gives it a peck,
She helps to keep the squirrel in check.

The squirrel tries to stare me down for some reason,
They get aggressive during mating season.

One day I saw the squirrel being chased by the bird,
She called for help and her cry was heard.

Mockingbirds came swooping down from everywhere,
The squirrel had to leave from there.

They chased it across the yard and into an oak tree,
The squirrel was safe and home free.

Thanks, little Mockingbird for all your help,
Now that squirrel will watch its step.

The Stray Dog

I cannot go to the mailbox without seeing a dog,
Some days they are thick as fog.

On any given day you will see all different kind,
Some things they do boggles the mind.

It looks like my lawn is the only place they poop,
Last week I had to go buy a scoop.

You must carry a stick to keep them from biting,
Sometimes in the street dogs be fighting.

One day I watched a red stray dog walk by in a slow gait,
That little red dog almost met its fate.

The neighbor's big brown mutt came out of nowhere fast,
Even though one of its back legs had a cast.

Mutt was on red so fast he stopped and coward down,
Now little red by-passes our side of town.

Old Red found out the hard way that life can be hard,
Be alert when passing by another dog's yard.

The Chicken (fussing/clucking)

You know sometimes I hate myself for being a chicken,
Hawks think we're easy picking.

That old sorry rooster just stands outside and gawk,
He's a prime target for the hawk.

We are raised and fed by a peddler named Percy,
He shows that rooster too much mercy.

The way other hens and roosters treat me is not fair,
It must be something in the air.

There was a hen who thought she was smart, named Cat,
I kept telling her she was getting too fat.

One day Percy picked her up and said she was a winner,
She was plucked for Sunday dinner.

I told those lazy hens they better stop laying around,
Chickens have no stand your ground.

Whether it be a fox or old man Percy that I meet,
I'm the fastest yardbird on two feet.

Old Pete The Stubborn Mule

A mule's life is hard, and we are never cut any slack,
If not plowing, there's a saddle on my back.

Day in and day out I am always under the gun,
On my rest day I'm too tired for fun.

Every morning little Ike gets the harness off the wall,
Old Pete must answer the call.

There were little Ike, big Ike and I did not like either one,
They ate lunch but didn't give me none.

One morning little Ike came, I said, today I'm not going,
Big Ike came stomping and blowing.

I guess the old man thought little Ike had been funning,
After hearing me talk he took off running.

I rolled over and was proud to have stood my ground,
This is one mule that doesn't play around.

I was walking around strutting all proud and glad,
Then I woke up, it was only a dream I had.

The Wildlife

Here we go again with these tourists hiking on my beat,
They can't outrun me with just two feet.

They never see the sign that says do not feed the wildlife,
I'm a Bobcat and my teeth are sharp as a knife.

I have lots of friends in the woods and one is a bear,
He's big and he doesn't play fair.

The tourist be smelling loud after taking a bath,
We can smell them miles up the path.

Some will not follow rules and keep their windows up,
They like to feed us from a cup.

Some even try to treat us like we are their pet,
Those are the ones who haven't learned yet.

Some will go riding off by themselves on a hike,
Thinking that they're safe on a bike.

It's time for this bobcat to crawl out of bed,
Maybe by a tourist I'll be fed.

I Am Back, The Runt

You remember me, the little dog that was born a runt,
The one on whom them cats pulled a stunt.

I will show them now, I got my friends Bill and Willie,
We're going to make that tomcat look silly.

They must put up the dukes or put them feet down,
Today there's a new sheriff in town.

We are going to see if them felines going to chuckle,
When that tomcat tastes my knuckle.

Here they come, I stepped up, squared off for the fight,
I looked back, Bill and Willie were nowhere in sight.

I knew I should have gone by and got old crazy Jack,
At least he would've had my back.

It's a good thing that I stopped by my friend Frasier,
He convinced me to take his taser.

Them cats will not be coming around here anymore,
I left them screaming and twitching on the floor.

Now I know who I can depend on when things get chilly,
I do know it's not Bill and Willie.

Little Otis

I live on the outskirts of the City and I'm a mouse,
My home is in the corner of a brick house.

I must be careful when I go out into the front yard,
Teddy the cat is always on guard.

Teddy chases me every time I step outside,
There aren't many places to hide.

That old silly cat is just a big dumb sap,
I read him every day like a map.

I laid under a tree and one eye open I was to be keeping,
He sneaked up and caught me sleeping.

I told him if he put salt on a bird's tail it was easy picking,
And it tastes like country fried chicken.

One time while running I slipped and fell,
He caught me by my tail.

I told him I knew where he could catch a big juicy rat,
And without thinking he fell for that.

The Lumpy Baseball

Look glove, I have been hit so hard it's not funny,
The league should be paying me money.

All you do is hang around on somebody's hand,
I get hit into the stand.

You rest on a hip or side and play catch,
Out of me they knock a patch.

I've been hit into the pole and out of the park,
Sometimes I'm even hit after dark.

I have been bunted and sometimes hit hard,
I have even landed in a fan's yard.

All over me that Louisville slugger has left its mark,
Some have game and some just bark.

When I am moving fast some players will slide,
Sometimes in a glove I'll hide.

Pitchers use me in curves and breaks to strike a player out,
Sometimes I make the managers shout.

When I'm a grand slam it makes the batter proud,
It also excites and pleases the crowd.

It's time for me to heal my bump and my bruise,
I'm going on a one-way cruise.

Slugger The Baseball Bat

Say glove, why did you let that catcher get hit in the eye?
You even let a pop up get by.

You're not that good anyway you may as well admit,
Today I'm going to make you quit.

I did not come here to chat with you or play the dozen,
I came to hit that ball for splitting my cousin.

That ball is going to find out why they call me slugger,
I can also be used on a mugger.

The other day they stopped me from hitting in the rain,
On that ball I was ready to inflict pain.

One day I hit a ball past a guy and made him think twice,
He found out that I'm nothing nice.

There was the time I blasted a ball from Texas to Poland,
It hit a farmer causing his eye to be swollen.

I hit a ball so hard a guy trying to catch it turned a flip,
He fell on his face and busted a lip.

One morning I hit a fast ball straight out of the park,
It didn't hit the ground until after dark.

I made a believer out of the little guy on third base,
I'm the greatest slugger, I rest my case.

The Mosquito

A mosquito is little, but it wreaks havoc day and night,
When stepping outside be ready to fight.

It hides until you step out and become a blood bank,
Into your skin the blood sucker sank.

Trying to sleep, all through the night you hear it buzz,
Whispering in your ear calling you Cuz.

I have tried everything except sleeping under a net,
It hasn't come to that yet.

There is this one little mosquito that I can barely see,
Night after night it won't let me be.

That little pest is becoming a pain in my side,
In the daytime it run and hide.

At the family picnic the mosquitos hit and run,
Taking away from the fun.

I went to the store and bought a can of bug spray,
I'm determined to put that mosquito away.

The Little Gnat

I may be little, but I can make a human being cry,
All I need to do is get in the eye.

One thing for sure as being a pest goes,
I can fly into the nose.

I am glad that I'm not big like a fly or a mouse,
I can easily fly into the house.

I really am not like a blood sucking mosquito that bite,
Why do people put up such a fight?

Swatting at me is not like hitting that little ball off the tee,
I'm almost too small to see.

Sometimes I hang around people who have food,
I can make them change their mood.

There was this one guy who fooled me with a trick,
I wish I could lift a brick.

I guess it's time for this little gnat to fly away,
Live to be pesky another day.

Drunk Man Passing By

Sometimes it's funny watching a drunk man walking,
Some are quiet and some be talking.

They will walk 3 or 4 steps, stop, and look all around,
Then some will sit on the ground.

One guy never makes it home, he sits in a driveway,
This is his routine every day.

After he makes a couple of steps, he looks up at the sun,
He's sweating and not having fun.

Then he looks around to find a grassy spot in the shade,
Now he figures he's got it made.

One day an ambulance came and took him for a ride,
The next day he had a cane by his side.

Yesterday he was drunk and staggering just like before,
Today he's headed back to the store.

Looks like he is starting off today a little late,
He's walking at a slow gait.

I hate to see the little man ruining his life that way,
Hopefully, he'll sober up one day.

The Bossy Hen

Let me see, let's look at this little hen, Alberta today,
Always scratching around no eggs do she lay.

She likes telling all the other hens and roosters what to do,
Pip said she's the first to run if you say boo!

Jane and Verdell said how she was always clucking,
Sara said that her feathers needed plucking.

Big Mama came by and asked had they heard the scoop,
Walter was thinking about putting her in a soup.

Now because of Alberta being a tough old hen,
Walter thought about selling her to Ren.

Ziah said that Ren did not need her because he had hogs,
If O'Neal got her she'd be chased by dogs.

To Joe and Mr. Junior, Walter made a long-distance call,
Junior said the hen couldn't feed them all.

Abe and Preacher bought her and decided to clip her wings,
Now the hen just lays around and sings.

Orel and Potner stole the little hen from Abe and Preacher,
Took her to school and sold her to the teacher.

The kids like to tease her and feed her some bread,
Alberta is happy so nothing more is said.

Rooster Trouble

Perk was a pint size rooster who thought he was a king,
On the farm old man Ike let Perk do his thing.

Mr. Buddy and Irene hated when he slept on their roof,
They told Mr. Ike but he wanted some proof.

Lonnie lived on the same street as his brother Baby Joe,
Billy Farmer and Mack said that Perk had to go.

Perk was fast, his wings were not clipped, so he could fly,
Flying over Mr. George he dropped a bird pie.

Mr. Zeke and his wife Myrtle lived on a dead-end road,
Perk rested on their roof after chasing a toad.

Mrs. Lottie told Hattie to holler if she sees Perk coming,
Shirley was boiling water and humming.

Mrs. Thelma, Mrs. Ella and Aunt Bea stopped by,
Emma cutting onions was starting to cry,

Mr. Boy caught Perk, carried him to Mrs. Lottie in a sack,
Perk pecked Hattie and flew out the back.

Perk finally made his way back to the farm,
He had narrowly escaped bodily harm.

After almost becoming chicken soup in Mrs. Lottie's pot,
Perk slept safely in the barn on a little cot.

The Roaming Bulls

There were young bulls in Korhville sowing their wild oats,
They moved so fast it was hard to take notes.

One bull that kept up a ruckus was turned into a rooster,
We'll have to use Butt as a booster.

Butt was a Brahman bull that was humble and had no fear,
If you teased him, you better put your feet in gear.

Nook and Jake, two smaller young bulls grazed together,
With Yogi and Rodney, they were tough as leather.

The young bulls like Art, Morris, Jerry, Bill and Bubba Mack,
The old bulls took up their slack.

On breaking out the pen the young bulls were exempt,
The old bulls made the first attempt.

Lloyd, Tee and Chubby were roaming out in the same field,
They ate Mr. Marshall's corn, so he got no yield.

Koochie, Lump and Titus were bulls that jumped the fence,
Wilford and Donnie had better sense.

Marvin was a wise bull that knew how to open a latch,
He got into Mr. Square's watermelon patch.

Mr. O'Neal had 3 Angus bulls that kept running away,
He fed them corn so they would stay.

The Pretty Little Pullets

Korhville had a few but not too many little pullets,
A rooster had to be careful or dodge bullets.

The farmers and their wives kept an eye on their flock,
They took turns around the clock.

Jake the rooster was tipping around trying to be slick,
Until the day he heard that shotgun click.

Now old Jake has a new name, they call him Hoppy,
He got shot in the toe by a farmer called Poppy.

There was another rooster on the yard named Bay,
He liked Martha and saw her every day.

Hoppy and Bay thought they were big time players,
They were shunned by the gainsayers.

Suddenly, Bay stopped crowing for a long time,
Poppy sold him while he was in his prime.

Tolson had 3 pullets, and visiting them you didn't try,
That bull whip would make a rooster cry.

Playing Cowboys And Indians

I remember when we'd go out and cut a green stick,
The best one we would pick.

We tied a hay string around the fat part,
Then the fun would start.

Away we would go on our stick horses running,
For bad guys we'd be gunning.

On our side we had a trusty six shooter,
Back then no one had a scooter.

Some of the boys had an old potato sack,
They placed it on the stick's back.

We would be shooting as we rode that stick,
With a strap we gave our backside a lick.

Cowboys and Indians is the game we played most,
We tied our stick horses to a wooden post.

Running down that dirt road kicking up dust and sand,
Playing Cowboys and Indians was grand.

Memories is all I have of those days since I became a man,
I go to the country as often as I can.

Tell Me Something Feet

You really don't want to hear what we have to say,
It would take us more than a day.

We have been a lot of places that we can't talk about,
If we talked, the Church would get up and shout.

We walked on land in London and Germany overseas,
Stuff that we know will knock a mule to his knees.

We have walked barefoot in the sand and a berry patch,
Came through the briars without a scratch.

We made a living pressing the fuel pedal on a big truck,
Walked through mud and never got stuck.

We walked in clubs and danced in rowdy bars,
Pressed the pedal on a few cars.

We walked in places we should have never been,
A lot was going on in our life back then.

Today we are tired and aged and for soft shoes we search,
Now we walk in fellowship at Church.

Tomorrow we will lay in because we have lost our pep,
Getting out of bed we must watch our step.

Willie The Raccoon

My name is willie and I'm an easy-going raccoon,
I don't like getting up before noon.

People look at me when I grin and think that I am mean,
I'm just showing them that my teeth are clean.

A lot of people say that I'm quick tempered and rude,
They destroyed my home looking for that crude.

There is this old man and it is me that he hunts,
But I'm prepared with my tricks and stunts.

Looks like today the old man brought with him a dog,
I might shake them running across this log.

I must try something else because that didn't work,
I think that old dog is just being a jerk.

It's time I showed them that they can't out fox Willie,
I'll make them both look silly.

I ran through the water so my scent they couldn't follow,
Now, I'm safely home balled up in my hollow.

I usually don't go out in the morning, I wait until night,
With my bad back I must avoid a fight.

Horace The Lion

I am a lion, king of the jungle and its nature's way,
My name is Horace don't vex me today.

Today I hope Jerry, Billy and I do not meet,
Those two warthogs I'm going to eat.

There are 3 buffaloes that graze near a grass patch,
Harry and Promise are hard to catch.

There's one little gazelle called Jim who try to be slick,
Catching him should be quick.

Pride let's go find some food, that is the magic word,
Let's separate Lonnie or Johnny from the herd.

Coke, you better be careful I saw a poacher with a gun,
They got Dennis because he couldn't run.

I am strong and prey cannot escape my locked jaw,
I can split prey in half with just one paw.

I am an Alpha male and I'm the king of this castle,
Nobody can give me any hassle.

I am a king, and everybody trembles when I roar,
They'll never bother me anymore.

The Sitting Duck

I fly around and swim in lakes minding my own business,
I walk and run for physical fitness.

A lot of my friends stay too long out on the lake,
Sometimes it's their last mistake.

Some think that they are invincible and fly too low,
To the hunter their belly will show.

We all know whenever we hear a loud pop,
One of us is sure to drop.

Some of the old hunters will use a fake bird call,
Just to mount a duck on their wall.

I was flying over a small lake and saw this mallard hen,
I was thinking maybe she would share my den.

Then I heard a pop and thought I had run out of luck
The hunter had planted a wooden duck.

Well, it is time for this duck to pack up and head south,
Fly by and drop some used bird seeds in his mouth.

The Crazy Cow

I'm a cow and I don't live on old MacDonald's farm,
I'm not flattered by your charm.

I am a Texas Jersey milk cow named Susie,
The man who owns me is a doozy.

The barn that he keeps us in is crumbling down,
The bull here is a first-class clown.

When I see old man Tena coming in with a pail,
I try to slap him with my tail.

He pats me on my back for milk trying to be slick,
Sometimes I'll give him a swift kick.

I watched and learned how to open the gate too,
It's amazing the things I can do.

I watched through the window when he was making butter,
Inside the farmer's house was a clutter.

He calls me ornery and crazy, but I have good sense,
I'm tired of being behind this fence.

The Pole Cat

I'm that black and white thing that you call a skunk,
To my mate I'm a handsome hunk.

Some people call us polecats bless their soul,
Have you ever seen a skunk up a pole?

Never surprise me and make me raise my tail,
You will not like the smell.

Know that seeing me, does not make me your pet,
If you poke me, a surprise you'll get.

There was this one guy who I accidently sprayed,
In his truck he should have stayed.

What do you expect when you come into our woods?
Contaminating and destroying our goods.

I will be a polecat if that's the name you choose,
But if you surprise me, you'll lose.

Let me give you some darn good advice if I may,
If you see me coming run away

The Dollar Bill

In a fast-paced world, what about the dollar bill?
It goes up and down hill.

Money is a must have and without it you will struggle,
It's hard when two jobs you're trying to juggle.

With the right amount of money, you can buy a lot,
You can also put meat in the pot.

Some people will stash some money away,
Keeping it for a rainy day.

There are some who like to lay around and chill,
Never saving, not one-dollar bill.

Some like to buy a big house and a fancy ride,
Others send money overseas to hide.

The dollar bill has been around for a long time,
I spent a lot during my prime.

For the dollar bill the road has already been paved,
How many dollars have you saved?

The Squeaky Chair

Not one to talk but it has been brought to my attention,
There's something that I must mention.

You pretend not to know what's going on when we squeak.
That is how the chairs speak.

Some have sat in me and my springs were broken,
Jumped up without a word being spoken.

Kids sit in me while they drink milk and cookies,
Some athletes who use me are rookies.

There are some who are heavy and some who are light,
If you going to sit in me do it right.

There's a critter that scratches me called a dog,
Wish I could hit him with a fire log.

To the next one who sits in me I will not be so kind,
It's time for this chair to unwind.

I have been sat on more than once with a broken leg,
Maybe that dog can teach me to beg.

The Talkative Schoolhouse

A lot of people have passed through my revolving door,
Many feet have walked this floor.

Come on in and chat awhile, have a seat,
Take a load off your feet.

I can tell stories about kids who hung out in the halls,
About writings on the bathroom walls.

There are those who come into the classroom yearning,
With a goal to achieve higher learning.

There are those who come to school that are lazy,
They do things that are crazy.

One time I saw a big bully picking on a little kid,
Let me tell you what I did.

I opened a little hole in my roof and made a water spot,
The bully slipped and got a head knot.

I am not here for just amusement and recreation.
I'm here for their education.

The Angry City Bus

If you had to go through what I go through every day,
You would feel the same way.

There are some people who try to board me without paying,
My on-time trips they're delaying.

Rowdy passengers keep the driver all stressed out,
Especially when they scream and shout.

Some are known to get physical with the driver,
Today's guy is a brave survivor.

Every day I encounter drunkards who argue and cuss,
In the back they keep up a fuss.

I must put up with cars ducking out and cutting in,
How am I supposed to win?

There is one driver who drives too fast and make mistakes,
Following too close and jamming the brakes.

Tonight, I'm going to let the tires go flat,
We'll see how he likes that.

Johnny Rabbit

My name is Johnny and I am a rabbit,
I do things out of habit.

It's hard for me to get into the carrot patch,
The gate has a metal latch.

Farmer Brooks had an old dog named Ray,
I could outrun him any day.

It looks like he has been to the dog pound,
He returned with a new hound.

I hope I don't have go to war with this clown,
I wonder what he's putting down.

The carrots are tasty and does my body good,
If only the latch was made of wood.

Around here I am the fastest rabbit on four feet,
No one faster you will meet.

Tonight, I will teach that new dog a lesson,
Introduce him to Smith and Wesson.

Somebody Get That Woodpecker

They must have cancelled the bounty on that woodpecker,
I used to be taller than a double decker.

Because of that bird I have lost the top of my head,
Any other tree would be dead.

I used to be a lovely oak tree proud and tall,
Today another limb will fall.

Back in the old days they paid men a hefty bounty,
Woodpeckers were hunted in every county.

I guess by the birds, human laws have been jacked,
All over my body I'm being hacked.

Every time I hear that old pesky bird's wings flap,
My hopes are that it's caught in a trap.

I know somebody hear it hammering on me all day,
I be hoping they come and chase it away.

Maybe it is time for me to offer my own reward,
It's pecking on me a little too hard.

With all the holes in my body I am slowing dying,
To get rid of him I must keep trying.

I keep calling for help, but no one is coming,
Into the wind I'm just humming.

The Wise Goat

You know I did not live to get this old being a fool,
I know what is not cool.

These young Billy goats think that they know it all,
They're headed for a great fall.

I keep telling these nuts they better go on a diet,
Why do you think the farmer is so quiet?

I remember when I tried to warn my buddy Lump,
He was last seen being tied to a stomp.

Last year the same thing happened to that young goat Rob,
They put him on the pit with corn on the cob.

I keep telling them that some people put us on pits,
To live long you must use your wits.

I saw old Scooter get put on a stick over a fire to roast,
The next time we saw Scooter he was toast.

As for me, oh yeah, by the way, they call me little Bill,
I learned to lay low and chill.

What We Eyes Have Seen

Let us see, where do we begin, we been here and there?
These eyes have been everywhere.

We have traveled all over and we been a lot of places,
We have seen frowns, sad and happy faces.

The other day we saw a man with a bad demeanor,
His language could've been cleaner.

There was a girl who winked but we didn't wink back,
She was with a tough guy named Mack.

There are a lot of ways these two eyes get into trouble,
Getting hit by Wilford will have you seeing double.

Going down those long dark country roads at night,
We must use man made light.

Sometimes the left eye gets crossed up and confused,
Makes this right eye feel like I'm being used.

We have camped in the woods and gazed at the stars,
Even been burned in smoked filled bars.

We traveled around and stretched ourselves to the max,
Now it's time for these eyes to relax.

What Do Blue Jeans Talk About?

Okay now blue jeans be careful what you say,
You know how the world is today.

Today it is hard just talking and having a friendly word,
You get sued by people for what they heard.

We don't care, she knows she cannot fit into a size ten,
She has burst jeans at every store she's been.

Like the guy who thinks he looks good in skinny jeans,
Please let me tell him, go ahead by all means.

You pass by a store with sizes no higher than a twenty-four,
You wear a 36, don't touch that door.

Some girls cannot walk because we are too tight,
Causing their legs to get into a fight.

Then some cut us off shorter than a miniskirt,
Okay no more dishing out dirt.

Now wait a minute girl you know that is not right,
Stepping out in jeans that are too tight.

So that you can walk right, run if need to, bend and sit,
Please buy some jeans that fit.

The Untamed Tongue

So, you thought that I would adhere to the letter,
Your parents should know better.

In me I have the power of death and life,
I'll cut through you like a knife.

Did not the Lord give you a Book of instructions?
I have caused many destructions.

With just the tip of me many have lied,
Because of me many have died.

I flatter men and women with just the right word,
I make sure that I'm heard.

I am known to cause one to stutter, (when lying)
Deceit flows from me like butter.

Parents should teach you about me in your youth,
I have no friendship with the truth.

Trying to tame me could be worth a try,
I can break and make you cry.

Though I may be little, and I may be small,
I can make the rich and powerful fall.

Lazy Rabbit

A lot of the rabbits think that I am trying to run a game,
Let me introduce myself, Shorty is my name.

Some of the rabbits think that I am dumb and lazy,
I refuse to get up when it's raining or hazy.

They keep talking about the squirrel that was almost shot,
How he was almost dinner in a pot.

Now don't get me wrong I am not really hating,
Some rabbits are doing a lot of fabricating.

Like the time Terry rabbit said he jumped over the moon,
And made it back home just before noon.

An old school rabbit from the country farm named Square,
Said that in love and war all is fair.

For the most part to hang with them I am thrilled,
But a lot of stuff they say will get you killed.

A lot of the old timers are wise and very cool,
They didn't get old being a fool.

Rule is, believe half of what you see, none of what you hear,
Be careful who you lend your ear.

So Now You Want To Ride My Back

Okay, so you could not ride the bucking bull,
What are you trying to pull?

I am smarter than any old bull, you will see,
I have got bucking down to a tee.

It's not enough the bull threw you and you got hooked,
If you get on me your goose is cooked.

If you straddle my back it will be an unforgettable ride,
Clowns see me coming they run and hide.

There are other crazy men just like you who have tried,
Hitting the ground, like a baby they cried.

There has got to be a better way for you to earn a living,
Easy rides this horse isn't giving.

I noticed that some of you cowboys like to chew or dip,
Riding me, I will bust your hip.

I am curious, you could not stay on the bull's back,
Do you think I will cut you some slack?

You will be better off trying to ride an old Hinny,
Riding me, you will not make a penny.

The Rodeo Calf

It is officially opened, it's that time of the year,
Time for me to get in gear.

I am a top Rodeo calf and my name is Ricky,
Dodging that rope can be tricky.

I had to grow up fast and learn to be slick,
With my feet I must be quick.

I have seen how they roped calves in the past,
For them slowpokes I'm just too fast.

You cannot do to me what you did to Chester,
He was my great Ancestor.

I am going to make you look like a little squirt,
Today you'll be eating my dirt.

A word to the wise, if you want to get over the hurdle,
Go rope a slow turtle.

Yesterday I made your nag look like a fool,
Today you'll join that pool.

Do not be too embarrassed because I was just too fast,
Horses quicker than yours didn't last.

I'm going back inside and get a well-deserved rest,
Now you know I am the best.

The Retired Belt

Finally, my old owner decided to retire me,
She's not like she used to be.

The little old lady that own me, they call her granny,
She used to work as a nanny.

Granny believed in correcting children with her belt,
She could spank without leaving a welt.

From the first time she took me off the wall,
I have witnessed and done it all.

I remember the day that she picked me out in the store,
She wanted a belt thicker than the one before.

Sometimes she would wear me around her waist,
I even saw her take a little taste.

She used to wake her son by hitting him on his backside,
Hearing her coming he would hide.

Granny even put me on the dog to use as a collar,
Her grandson tried selling me for a dollar.

I was tied around the post on the backyard gate,
She used me on grandpa when he came in late.

Granny retired from work and is relaxing as she should,
Now I'm hanging on the wall for good.

The Runaway Dog

Whew! I finally got a break and found a way out,
I'll see what freedom is about.

My name is Morris and I am a little dash hound,
I'm headed westward bound.

For a long time, I was cooped up in that yard,
Every night I was on guard.

They say that man's best friend is supposedly a dog,
Why do I have to root for food like a hog?

I broke out of there and I am never going back,
They never did cut me any slack.

Hey now, it's looking good, I hope a tree is near,
Where do they keep the beer?

There go a couple of dogs running around free,
I'll stop and mark this tree.

Hey! wait a minute, what are they chasing me for?
Wow! I almost got hit by a car.

I have only been out for a minute and I'm already in a fix,
Me and the outside world may not mix.

I been chased by other dogs, and by a car I was almost hit,
I better get back in the yard where I fit.

Old Folks Do The Darndest Things

I was looking for my glasses all over the place,
There they were on my face.

While talking to my sister I was looking for my phone,
She said, "what are you talking on?"

Then you go into another room and just like that,
You forget what you went at.

Just like a child who sneak out the house to go play,
The mind sometimes wonders away.

You write yourself a short do not forget note,
You lose it and forget what you wrote.

You go to the store and forget what you went after,
You tell your friends much to their laughter.

You cause your phone to get stuck in the lock mode,
Uh oh, you forgot the code.

Our children are always buying us memory food,
Not every day are we in a good mood.

Well I better move on before my memory gets lost,
Probably can't get it back without a cost.

The Old Pesky Ant Again

I know you thought I was gone but here I am,
Across this yard we're building a dam.

They call us fire Ants, because we can make it hot if we try,
Enough of us can make anybody cry.

Today we bit a couple and made them act like a clown,
Neighbors thought it was a country hoe down.

I hear what you are saying, we know it's your yard,
But our Queen we must guard.

When you pick a spot to plant and you see our hill,
Please be kind and don't till.

If intruders start destroying your home you'll fight,
Intrude on us and we'll bite.

A lot of times we will build our home under a tree,
Just like you we're born free.

When you're cutting your yard and you see a mound,
Do not disturb us go around.

Just so you know when you use that smelly bleach,
We go deep far out of reach.

Maybe we can find a way to put all this behind us,
Just be cool and stop making a fuss.

The Super Trucker

I've been running the road with this guy for a long time,
We been together since his prime.

My name is Pete, it's short for the truck, Peterbilt,
I have a steering wheel that can tilt.

You know they call my driver super for a reason,
He drives fast in and out of season.

Please do not ride with us if you are timid,
He drives above the speed limit.

I remember the day he caused me to lose my nerve,
At a 100 mph he took a curve.

Let me tell you little four wheelers a thing or two,
He is geared to run over you.

Read the signs and stay off his blind side,
You might keep that pretty ride.

Please don't get in front of us going down a hill,
You'll get more than a chill.

The Super Trucker does not go by rule and regulation,
He has earned his reputation.

The Big Ego

Just so you know, I started out the size of a small fig,
Now some are saying that I've grown too big.

If you don't like what I do don't step in my ring,
I'm one who does my own thing.

Let me tell you something, I don't listen to nobody,
You need to go somewhere and sit on a potty.

I been building myself up for an awfully long time,
I 've had this big head since my prime.

I know you think I'm getting too big for my britches,
Just because my car runs others into ditches.

Uh oh, look like you were right, my head was too big,
I lost my good job and part time gig.

I must back track and apologize for the way I acted,
I didn't realize all the lives I impacted.

Now that you have shown me, I see, and I know.
I never should've catered to my ego.

I walk around all day with my head hanging down,
Now I'm the one who looks like a clown

War

The First Gulf War (back to Iraq)

Listen up, it was not another war like Viet Nam,
All they could hear were bombs going bam!
Our leaders did not have to take a risk,
And send in a rushing blitz.

While our fighter planes were in the sky,
Our flag was flying high.
The smart bombs were bursting in the air,
Bombs were bursting everywhere.

The enemy troops had no place to hide,
They had to take a ride.
We sent them quickly running back to Iraq,
With having no time to pack.

Of our plans he must not have been told,
We had two aces on hold.
In one hand we had straight air power,
Every minute of the hour.

In the other hand, we had elite ground troop,
We put an end to his coup.
Giving up with the sadness of a beaten frown,
They laid all their weapons down.

Our leader was a strong firm handed man,
He used a bullet proof plan.
The President deserved to get a high five,
He brought the boys back alive.

Our leader was dealing the cards true and fair,
He dealt the opponent two pair.
We went in and took the Country back.

The Second Gulf War

It was inevitable so this war had to come,
Although it seemed wrong to some.
Put yourself in the tortured people's place,
Look in the mirror at your face.

Living where evil was able to dictate,
Was a lot of people's fate.
Their cry for freedom rang loud and clear,
An evil dictator they did fear.

Opening her heart America answered the call,
The evil dictator had to fall.
Of his own people he had killed many,
Compassion he did not show any.

He was killing his people at the drop of a hat,
No just man could stand for that.
He did people wrong we went in to make it right,
We hit him with missiles in the night.

The surprise attack put him and his sons on the run,
Dodging bombs was not fun.
They were chased from town and out of the city,
For them there was no pity.

The sons were cornered but did not want to be tried,
At them, a hail of bullets was fired.
For the evil dictator, many days they would look,
Trying to close a chapter in the book.

For the evil dictator they were looking everywhere,
In a spider hole they found him there.
It was the end of his dictating career.

Drugs

Drugs Woes

The town was happily booming and growing,
One day drugs started Flowing.

Cocaine was his name and he had an offspring,
Smoking crack was their thing.

Alcohol and tobacco had caught a very solid grip,
People wanted to take a higher trip.

Maryjane was a drug weed already on the rise,
Snaring people who were not wise.

Drugs are downing people from high places,
Being ashamed to show their faces.

The drugs do not have a color line or barrier,
Anyone can be a carrier.

Hooking the weak and the strong is their aim,
Pain and death are their game.

Whatever you do please take heed,
Illegal drugs you don't need.

Life or Drugs

Early each morning I kneel-down and I pray,
To resist temptations each day.

I give a man a day's work for the money he will pay,
Then I'll be on my way

I strive to live a very peaceful and drug free life,
I'm happy with my children and wife.

You must be careful of the road you choose,
Doing drugs, you're sure to lose.

Drugs are destroying lives and killing each day,
Why do so many go that way?

Drugs rob the poor and gives to the fast and greedy,
Taking away from a family that's needy.

To your body be careful what you give,
If a long life you're desiring to live.

Life is a precious gift to us from the Lord,
We can make it easy or hard.

Once Upon A Time In Korhville Texas

As I look back over my life growing up in the black settlement of Korhville Texas, let's see how I got there.

My first memory, as far back as I can, was when I was between the age of 3 and 4. One thing that stands out in my mind is the day a bull got loose in the camp. The camp was a place, make-shift community where the black men and their families lived while the men were out doing construction work and working on the railroad, it was called the Humble camp. Basically, it was located between Tomball and Korhville Texas.

Of course, the land belonged to the whites that the men were working for and there were cattle on the land. Although the animals were fenced in separately from the living quarters of the families, every now and then a bull would get out and roamed the area of the housing where the people lived and terrorized the women and children. Now all the women could do was wait for the men to come home from work and pen up the bull or try to chase it back to the pasture from where it had come from, which was very dangerous.

One day when a bull got out, I had crawled up on a ladder that was outside leaning on the little wooden and tin shack that we were living in on the camp.

I remember a woman running out hollering for me to "stay there, don't move!" She ran over picked me up and climbed on top of the house and stayed up there with me until the bull passed by and left the area.

The camp was not always peaceful, my father was abusive toward my mother, for whatever reason, one was, he drank a lot, got drunk. One time he started to hit my mother and he had a stroke. When he raised his hand to hit her, the stroke happened. My mother was a praying, God fearing woman. We would always hear her praying day and night.

Well, my mother stepped out on faith with her children beside her and left that abusive situation with nothing but clothes, her kids and faith, not knowing where we would stay, what we would eat. I remember walking down that long dark, dirt road, Hufsmith-Korhville road, heading to Korhville.

That was a very scary road, there was a real dark section of road down by willow creek with a raggedy bridge that we had to cross. The bridge squeaked and made a lot of noise. You could hear animals in the woods running and stepping on twigs, leaves and stuff that was breaking as they walked and ran. I was the slowest one, and I would cry. My mother would tell me to stop crying and to come on and keep up. It was challenging, Korhville here we come.

It was the year of 1954 when my family and I arrived in the little black settlement of Korhville Texas, just north of Houston Texas, just a hoot and holler up the road from the camp, around the corner, down yonder, you get it.

Korhville Texas was a small community where former, newly freed slaves from Mississippi and Alabama came and settled. There were 7 streets, 4 main connectors, Spring Cypress road, West Montgomery road, Louetta and Hufsmith-Korhville road, which was the path to Hufsmith Texas, a few miles north of Korhville and just east of Tomball Texas. The 4 main streets inside the black community of Korhville itself were Carter, Cossey, Rogers and old Louetta road. West Montgomery, Spring Cypress, Louetta, and Hufsmith-Korhville road were the lifelines for the settlement.

West Montgomery road took the farmers and merchants to Houston Texas down to the farmer's market to sell their goods. It also brought buyers along the road to the makeshift stands where the children would stand and sell blackberries. The young men of Korhville would get up early in the morning, gather their buckets and sticks, buckets for the berries and sticks to run off the snakes that they encountered along the way. Most of the men in the settlement were farmers, some carpenters, some pulpwood haulers, some worked other jobs for the few whites that were in the area. dairy farms, corn fields, hoeing peanuts, digging potatoes, however, a lot of the men worked for themselves. Some had their own trucks and were hay haulers, well diggers, some were trash haulers. Every man worked hard and provided for his family and whenever needed, helped his neighbor.

Korhville had its own canning building, and when they were not canning food, the women would use the building to make quilts. They were not slothful people because they could not afford to be lazy. They built a Church and School, somehow the first School they built, it burned down. After all the dust settled and Korhville was back in the saddle, a new School and Church were built. I forgot to mention the Church burned down also, a coincidence, maybe? Naaaaw. When we left the camp and walked the 6 to 8 miles to Korhville Texas, there were 7 of us kids. 7 of us walking altogether including my mother, but only 6 of us children went to Korhville, one sister had left the camp and went to Louisiana with our grandma.

I was the only boy in the family, plus I was the baby in the family. One of the kind families in Korhville had a little store and gas station. They let us stay in it at night, free of charge, until we found a house which was supplied by one of the farmers in Korhville. That is just how friendly and neighborly the people of Korhville Texas were. The whites and the blacks were good neighbors to one another. Of course, there were places and people on the outskirts that were not so friendly, but within Korhville itself, the good outweighed the bad.

We ate at some of the same tables, swam in the same muddy creeks and sometimes worked together. The roads were dirt, thick sand that burned your bare feet in the summertime. There were 2 major corner stores in Korhville, each being on the main road from Acres Homes to Tomball, which was West Montgomery road. One was on the corner of West Montgomery and Hufsmith-Korhville road and the other one was on the corner of Spring Cypress and West Montgomery road. The store owners extended credit to the people of Korhville and we all became one big happy community during that period. We had ice boxes, no refrigerators, in which we had to buy a block of ice and put in the top of the ice box, where a freezer is in a fridge today and at the bottom was a pan to catch the water from the melting ice. Yes, it kept the food from spoiling, food did not spoil as quickly as it spoils today. We made our own butter, we churned milk to turn it into butter, it was a process.

They canned their own preserves, pear, peach, apple, fig, berry and plum jellies. They had smoke houses back then and they made sausages, ham, bacon and hog head cheese.

The smoke houses were filled with cured meat. A lot of the families had some farm animals such as chickens, cows, hogs, ducks, turkeys, guineas, horses and mules, and of course we ate everything except the horses and mules. Food was not wasted back then the way it is today, as parents today choose to allow kids to pick and choose what they will and will not eat. We had to eat whatever our mother cooked or go to bed hungry, but know this, if you chose to not eat and go to bed, that same plate of food was waiting for you the next day. Parents had rules that we had to obey and follow or suffer the consequences and the repercussion of our action and choices. They did not play with you if you broke their rules.

There were no short cuts when it came to obedience and respect. It was taught and instilled in us and we could not say that we did not know. If we did, we would be lying.

They didn't spare the rod, the whole community was your family and wherever you got out of line or acted up, that is where you were punished and by whoever saw you do whatever it was that warranted you a chastising. Thanks again to all the men and women pioneers of Korhville Texas that took me and my family in, in the year of 1954 and gave my mother a helping hand when she was a stranger and needed help. They took her and her children in as if we were their own. That is what having and stepping out on faith will do for you. Thanks for the memories Korhville, God is good, all the time. The farmers shared their goods with the people of the settlement, especially with those who were less fortunate. Corn, beans, potatoes, squash, okra and whatever was planted that was edible and they also shared meat whenever they butchered beef or pork. They were neighbors helping neighbors. Televisions and telephones were few to none and the ones that did have them, we were able to watch tv or make calls at the neighbors who had such things. The radio was the main source of information for the settlement of Korhville, and if you had a tv or phone, you were in high cotton.

To make a long story short, I am going to move along very rapidly, so if you do not mind, hang on and enjoy the ride. As I grew up and was going to school, I became friends with all the other boys in Korhville and in Hufsmith also.

I was popular with the elderly folks because I was a hard-worker and well-mannered young man. I chopped wood, dug flower beds, picked peas, dug potatoes, hoed peanuts and picked berries and helped the older people with any chores that they wanted me to do, even though some had children and grandchildren. I was known as Mrs. Latin's boy, ask him, he can do it and will do it. School was great, kids got a chance to see more of each other and got a chance to play together while being taught some of life's lessons. The teachers came from surrounding areas of Houston, like Garden City, Acres Homes, the Wards, Hufsmith and Tomball.

Summer was good for us, we could not wait to hear that school bell ring at 3:30 pm, time to go home. On the way home we would stop off in the woods and pick wild plums, huckleberries, muscadines, grapes, persimmons, berries, and wild cherries. We ate good out the woods back in the day and nobody bothered us, we were happy campers.

There was this one sad, dark day in Korhville where a young man was shot in the back as he ran to take cover in the store on Hufsmith-Korhville and West Montgomery road. He was my friend and an only child to his mother. He would stop by the house and help me chop wood, of course he was just showing off because he liked one of my sisters. He had said some words to a white man that the man did not take kindly to and the man got his rifle from his gun rack in the back window of his truck. You see, back then the white men were able to carry their rifles in their vehicles, in plain view or hid whichever, it was legal.

Well, anyway, the boy tried to run inside the store. The owner of the store wife saw what was happening and begged the white man not to shoot the boy, (she was white) but to no avail. The man shot him in the back and the boy died in his bed a year later, never, ever being able to walk again, he was paralyzed and bedridden until he died.

That was a sad day and no, nothing happened to the man who shot the boy, even though the woman from the store went to court and testified against him. That is how it was back in the day and we are still looking in that same mirror today and seeing similarities and worst.

So much for that, moving right along into the year of 1964, when the word of integration came to Korhville Texas.

Well we really supposed to had integrated in 1955 but they held it up to see what the government was going to do, it did not happen for us until 10 years later, 1965.

I was a teenager, 14 years old when we got the news about having to integrate , which meant being uprooted from our little black school that we loved and was used to and being bussed to an all-white school, Klein High School. We did not want to go, and we let our feelings be known. We rebelled at band practice one day chanting, "2-4-6 8, we don't want to integrate", led by Chubby,(Larry) and we all got a whupping from our principal for that little stunt. So much for that short-lived rebellion. As B.J. used to say, oh well.

That summer of 1965, we reluctantly went over and signed up for the school year, man we dreaded that day. It was about 15 to 20 of us boys from Korhville going to the high school and the rest went to the Junior high. The first year, maybe a year and a half, we fought daily, whether it was in the gym, classroom, hallway, on the bus, at games or off campus.

Not only did we have to fight the white boys from Klein, but we also had to fight the black boys being bussed in from a suburb of Houston, known as Garden City.

All and all we held our own and finally some of the white boys saw that we were brave and stood our ground, some started giving us money, being our friends, thinking we might help protect them from some of the guys from Garden City. Not everyone was on board, especially the older, more hard lined white boys. We were all boys at that time, so this by no means is any disrespect to no one or race, my using the word boy. We were considered boys or teens at that age. We were all between 15-17 years old at that time. So yes, we were boys.

As I look back over the years and times and I hear someone say, "those were the good old days", or "times were better back then", I look at each side of the coin. On one side, some things were good, but on the other side not good at all. Good were the foods, neighbors, parents, children, Church, family, morals and respect.

Bad were the times, separate Schools, backdoor restaurants, separate everything. The wages were low, men wrongfully accused, jailed, murdered, you name it.

No air condition, most families had a mule and wagon, or slide, some walked miles to school, learning from hand me down books, outdated books, learning everyone's history and culture but our own. We had an Ice box, no refrigerator, no fan, no tv and we went bare footed. We had mid-wives, no Doctor, no Hospital, no lawn mower. We used sickles and hoes, no carpet, some families had dirt floors, coal oil lamps, no electricity, wood stove, no gas or electric stove , hand saw and axe, no power tool, you get the picture. Be careful what you say and how you look down on people because you never know what they are going through or what they have been through. Be careful what you wish for.

Okay, now back to the story, I got a little side-tracked there for a minute. Some of the black guys played sports and were good at it, football, basketball and ran track. We were beginning to be accepted and started getting along a lot better, with the exceptions of a few. Although the majority seemed to have settled down and accepted us for what it was worth. Some fighting continued, but for the most part, the fights were few and in-between.

A few of us quit school because we did not like the idea of the white principal paddling us with his signature paddle and hearing the women in the office snickering and laughing when he was hitting us with that big hand-made paddle. My best friend and brother from another mother, he and I were more radical of all the boys from Korhville Texas or Garden City. Matter of fact, before we quit, the bus driver, who was white, tried to put me off the bus because of me mocking him, after he had said something to one of the white kids.

I repeated what he had said, and he got angry and all bent out of shape about it. It was raining, and we were half-way from the School and halfway from Korhville.

If that old girl from Garden City had not pointed me out, the outcome would have been different. Well, anyway, there is no way that, hold on, I am getting ahead of myself here. Okay, where were we? He had told a little white kid to sit down on the seat with me, he said "sit down boy, that boy is not going to bite you." I repeated what he said, he heard me and asked, "who said that"? No one was saying anything, then this black girl from Garden City spoke up and pointed me out. The bus driver tried unsuccessfully to make me get off the bus and walk home in the rain, 4 to 5 miles, are you kidding me? I would not and did not budge, so he turned the bus around and took us back to school. He went and got the principal, the counselor, and teachers, but they still could not talk me off the bus. They called the police, the police came on the bus, did not man handle me, they just talked. They knew me and my family, so eventually they talked me into getting off the bus. The next day I told my nieces who rode that same bus to tell the bus driver that he could not come to Korhville anymore. To make it look good and very convincing, the following day I went hunting, that is one of the activities that we did in the country. We would go squirrel, coon, rabbit, deer, and bird hunting, some even hunted armadillo. Any way, we could walk down the road with our shotgun or rifle with nothing said. It was all legal back then. I was out hunting and when it was time for the school bus to arrive that evening, I made my way out of the woods and towards the spot where the bus would be stopping to let my nieces off. When the bus reached the stop on the corner of Hufsmith-Korhville and Cossey road, I was emerging from the woods with my shotgun across my shoulder and I made sure the bus driver saw me. When he saw me, he almost took off with my nieces in the middle of the door getting off the bus. He left there in a hurry up mode. After that day, he quit that route and I never saw him again. We still laugh about that little incident today.

For the most part, Korhville, Klein and Garden City settled down and got to the business of enjoying School, accomplishing goals, and respecting each other. We maintained a good relationship with some of the people from Klein and Garden City who we had met during integration and the time spent in School together. We had fun and enjoyed life growing up in Korhville. We had teenage parties, we went camping in the woods, we played outside, not in the house, we went to Church every Sunday, sometimes on Friday or Saturday night and through the week, we could not say, no, I'm not going. We got whippings; the whole community helped raised you. They could chasten you too, nothing said and sometimes you had to go and cut your own switch. Kids were not killing parents, parents were not killing kids, people died of natural causes, living to a ripe old age. We respected our elders, we spoke to one another, we slept with our windows opened, we left doors unlocked. Sunday dinner was cooked on Saturday evenings and neighbors looked out for one another. When we were old enough, we worked. We had chores after school, we took off our school clothes time we got home after school and we had Sunday go-to meeting clothes and shoes that we didn't wear but to Church. Our parents bought us the necessities that we needed, nothing extra. If we wanted something extra or expensive, we had to get a job and buy it ourselves or do without, no ifs, ands or buts.

There are a lot of good things that happened in Korhville that I have not mention. I am mainly just touching on some of the things that happened while I was growing up in the black settlement of Korhville Texas. It was a great adventure and the Lord blessed me, my family and the people of Korhville. The families, the people, white and black were good neighbors. Our white neighbors were, the Naggis, Lacys, Jerdons, Straugans, Bells, Bominghaus, Saunders, Odoms, Waites, Walkers, Sellers, Hargraves, Cheakwoods, Rogers, Hesslers, Mannings, Turners, Beards, Woods and a few more I cannot remember but can see their faces, you know, they were all good neighbors.

The black families: Solomons, Cosseys, Blackshears, Williams, Curtis, Stewarts, Worthams, Whitfields, Jefferys, Greens, Hardys, Roundtrees, Latins, Horaces, Hogans, Tolsons, Hills, Lees, Blacks, Washingtons, Blantons, Lawerences, Mosleys, Calhouns, Amos, Barnes, Hubbards Pattersons, Woods, Carters, Singletons, Sims, Alexanders, Ramons, Autrys, Macks, Cloes, Moores, Rays, Jenkins, Fergusons, Lakeys, Suttons, Wests, Conleys, Allens, Browns, Johnsons, Petersons, Shennicks, Thomas, Buckners, Powells, Mr. Arthur B., Phillips, Smiths, Rufus, Bostics, Gibsons, Walkers, Morris, Farmers and the Chaneys.

I probably missed a few, but all and all, they were good neighbors and good people and still are today, them that are left and still there, even those that have moved and are still living, show their Korhville upbringing and hospitality. No place like Korhville Texas. No place.

Unforgettable Memories

Growing up in Korhville Texas was the greatest experience that I had as a kid. The people and the community were friendly and good neighbors. Back then, they had mid-wives who delivered babies and in Korhville there was one that I remember because she delivered one of my nieces, Mrs. Lottie was her name. Mrs. Lottie was a little short lady who dipped snuff and could outrun the fasted kid and she did not play. She was a great asset to the community. She was a pioneer for sure. We celebrated the Nineteenth of June every year. One of the men from the Whitfield family, Preacher, (Thomas Whitfield) and wife Marie, barbequed and invited the whole community and we would have a ball, yes sir. Neighbors shared their meats and vegetables and for the kids whose parents could not afford to buy them a Christmas present, the Good Fellas, a Non-profit group, stepped in and made sure we all got a present. The Good Fellas, of which the majority were our white neighbors. (some memories may mirror, once upon a time) At school we had Christmas plays and afterwards they gave out little Christmas bags with fruits and nuts in them. It was so wonderful and exciting for kids during those times.

The whole community helped in giving to the children and they all were more than glad to help to put a smile on our faces. For us kids, our main income was from selling black berries on the side of the main highway.

We had teenage parties at the YMCA, at one of the Solomon's and at Mrs. Susie Autry's house, whom we called, Aunt Susie. There was only one Juke Joint (Tee Hubbard's) during the early years and behind it, there was a baseball field where the grown-ups played baseball on Saturday or Sunday afternoons. Now in the later years, 2 more Joints popped up, by then they were calling them Cafes and Clubs, Molly's and Preacher's. My best years and best times in Korhville Texas, were between the years when I was age 6-30, because after that I got married and left, but I am still a regular there.

I went to the Army at age 20, trained in Fort Polk Louisiana, served in Germany and got a chance to visit London.

Some of the foreigners were anti-social in Germany and London. I discovered that prejudice was not just limited to American people, and that is a whole different book there, we are not going to open that chapter. Though I will say this, the Army let me down, failed me twice, once in Germany and once in Fort Hood, Killeen Texas. That happens when you're naïve. Let me move away from that, because if I told you what happened you would be upset too, but that is passed now and it is too late for me to do anything about it, and I did not have the resources back then. Yes, it brings back memories of tough times, so moving forward to much happier times. Let's just say that I am a survivor of hard times.

Later in my life, by becoming an over the road truck driver, I got a chance to visit 48 states and Canada. In my adult years, after the Army tour, I had stopped going to Church and by the time I reached 26 years of age I was shot, once at home and I was shot again at Molly's cafe. I carry 2 bullets in my back that reminds me every time I take an x-ray, technicians say "you know you have 2 slugs in your back" well yeah, duh? The bullets were too close to my spine for the doctors to remove, so it was best to leave them where they were. I am 70 and they are still there and giving me no trouble, plus I really cannot feel them or anything like that. No one, but God, thank you Lord for your Grace and Mercy. Amen.

Just giving a little insight to my life living outside of Church, God's plan, righteousness, and His Commandments.

Let me see, I was shot twice at 2 different times, by different people, I was run over twice, by 2 different tractors, I couldn't talk twice in my life, once because of being shot on the chin and the bullet traveling down my throat and once when I jumped off a fence post and my chin hit my knee and I bit my tongue off, it was hanging on by a thread. I ran in the house crying with my tongue in my hand. My mother just put it back in my mouth and told me to keep my mouth shut and I never went to, or ever saw a doctor for it. God at work.

I was falsely accused 3 times in my life, once by one of my sisters, got a whupping I did not deserve, once by an old lady, of being in the car with my cousin. My mother had said that she did not want me riding with him because he drove crazy and too fast. The lady told my mother she saw me in the car, when in fact it was one of the Hardy boys, Willie B, not me, but you were not allowed to defend yourself against an old person. That meant that you were calling an elderly person a lie and that was a big no.no, you could not do that.

I got a whupping for that, but the third time being falsely accused landed me in jail, but through it all, the Lord kept me from prison and out of the graveyard. I only spent a night in jail, so you see, I have a lot to thank God for. I thank God for a praying, God fearing mother and community, I thank God for keeping me out of prison and out of the graveyard. I thank God for His Grace and Mercy, I thank God for family, friends and good neighbors, I thank God for my lovely wife and sons, I thank God for retirement, I thank God for Medicare and Social Security, I thank God for a home and transportation, I thank God for the exercise gym, I thank God for all that He has done for me and is still doing for me and my family.

Being a husband and family man is a good thing, especially for me, it keeps me humble and I am enjoying life after retirement in my senior, golden years. I love going to

Church, working around the Church, assembling with the brothers, and fellowshipping with the people and I love a good game of dominoes. I consider myself the Texas Domino Champ, no brag, got Trophies to prove it. Yeah, I said it.

I enjoy serving the Lord and I enjoy life. This joy that I have now, the world did not give it to me, man did not give it to me, so man cannot take it away. Amen.

Through it all, the memories of growing up and living in Korhville Texas are good and if I had it to do all over again, Korhville is the place I would want to be and grow up. Where the fruit trees grew wild in the woods, we swam in ponds, creeks and gullies, camped in the woods without grown up supervision. Our parents knew that we were wise enough to look out for each other when we ventured out.

We made treehouses, shot marbles (game) played prairie football, made homemade ice cream, drank water from the well, ate meat straight out the smokehouse, summer sausage and crackers. Hog head cheese, chicken feet, respected our elders, did chores, and worked after school and on weekends. We ate homemade biscuits, homemade jelly, flap jacks and good ole Brer Rabbit syrup. We went to school within walking distance from our homes. There were two wooden buildings, with a principal and a teacher, but down through the years we had more than one teacher, most came from different places, such as Houston, Garden city, Hufsmith and Acres Homes. The ones who stayed the longest and were there until the closing of the school due to integration and bussing, were Mr. W.D. Richardson (principal) and his wife Mrs. Gladys Richardson our teacher. They were the greatest.

I remember one of the teachers, Mrs. Rayburn, she was a tough little woman. Freddie Williams got smart with her one day, he talked back to her. She told him that she would have her husband come to the school and throw him through that open window, she was angry with him. Back then kids stayed in a kid's place and we were not allowed to butt into grown folk conversations or talk back. Alright now Freddie.

We had three kinds of clothes, Sunday Church clothes, school clothes and last being play/work clothes, which was one and the same, because the clothes that you played in you also worked in. Through it all, teenage life was good for the kids in Korhville Texas. Moving right along, let us look at some of the bad boys of Korhville Texas during my time and teen era.

Now when I say bad boys, I am referring to two things, their cars and some for their fighting and bravery. I am going to name a few, but I am not going to talk about them all, because I cannot tell it all, there is not enough paper.

Let me see, I will start with the older guys first, like Woody, Tee, Freddie, Donnie, Terry, Boots, Wilford, David, Lump, JB, Herbert, Park, Lee Edward, Little Lloyd, Dave, Shorty, Artis, Jim, Titus, Harry, Mack, Melvin and Otha, Joe, Buddy, Willie, RL, John, Fox, Alexander, so many of them I can't mention them all. Some lived in Korhville and some lived in Cypress which was called, "the Woods," they were the rowdy bunch. They could make the whole place sit down and be quiet.

I saw it happen one night at Tee Hubbard's, the only beer joint in Korhville Texas at the time. It was one of the rowdy bunch. He walked into the place and unplugged the juke box and made everybody sit down and shut up. Yes, I sat down and was quiet as a Church house mouse, you did not even know I was in there. It's called, surviving the weekend.

One guy got hit upside the head with the rifle butt for not being quiet while he was sitting down at the bar. Yes sir, when the rowdy bunch had the floor you needed to find you a seat and be still or suffer the consequences of your actions.

Anyway, that is enough about the rowdy bunch who were known to raise a ruckus on weekends and sometimes through the week, if something was going down at a beer joint.

Do not get me wrong, they were all good people, just sowing them wild oats. Matter of fact, a lot of us boys worked for one of the rowdy bunch, and besides that, I was safe, he was my distance in-law in a way, because one of his brothers was married to one of my sisters. (Joyce Marie)

That sort of gave me a free pass, in-law privileges, yes it did.

Then there was an incident with Woody and Donnie, where they had gone to visit some friends in Acres Homes or Stude Wood, I forget which one, and oh yeah by the way, they had another friend with them. While they were inside the home some guys from the neighborhood walked up and waited for them to come outside, there were 9 guys. The guys broke the antenna on Donnie's car and after that, the fight was on, but the other guy who was with Donnie and Woody ran for help.
Of course, he said that he went to get some help, which to his credit he did bring back an old man who he ran across sitting outside on his porch. So, I guess he did save their bacon.
The old man did go and break up the fight, but by then Donnie had a tooth knocked out, Woody was bruised up with a black eye and swollen face. It could have been worse.
Then there was the time, Lump and Teddy got jammed up at Tee Hubbard's by some of the rowdy bunch's inner circle.
A guy put a razor to Teddy's throat, but Teddy managed to escape, and Lump and Teddy made it to Lump's house where Lump retrieved his rifle and got on the back of his truck.
Teddy drove, Lump told Teddy to "just ride me by", Lump was intent on shooting them up, but they could not find them. It was always touch and go at some of the beer joints between Korhville and Acres Homes, not to forget the Grove, Cunningham's and Teamer's, off old Jack Rabbit road.
At the time, beer was .25 cents a can, bottle, whatever you preferred, and cigarettes was .35 cents a pack and I cannot leave out that good old soda pop, which was .5 cents, a nickel. A dollar went a long way back then, just saying.
Now, on to us younger fellows, Perk, Jake, Butt, Yogi, Dan Bug, myself known as Nook, Hog, Tickle Britches (because he was always laughing), Cabbage, Bub, Pee Wee, Chubby, Jody, Big Moo, Plank, James Otis, David, Jeff, Joe, Beamer, Poochie, Koochie, Still Bill, Cecil, Jessie, Bubba M. Coke, Amp, Den, Duckbooty, Shine, Hamp, Don Ray, Jenks, August, Freddie 1, Freddie 2, Freddie 3, Freddie 4, yeah it was a lot of Freddies, and 4 James.
These were my running buddies, Perk, Butt, Jake, Yogi (BJ), Bubba (Terry) Boots, Beck, R.L, Little Lloyd, Herbert, Titus,

Dave, and Lump. These are the guys who I hung out with and went to beer joints with. Although Lump, Beck, Lank, Dave, Little Lloyd, Teddy, Park, Titus, Boots, Lee Edward, Bubba and Herbert were older than me, they took me under their wings and let me hang out with them.

Now hanging out at the beer joints was exciting, but it also had its dangers. Drunk men talking trash, wanting to fight, jealous boyfriends and losing gamblers. Yeah, it got crazy at times, I was shot at one café, got cut and had my share of fights at another. The weekends and Thursday nights got very wild, with a live band and beer raffles. Through it all, I made it through with the help of the Lord. Now had it not been for the Lord on my side, I would not have made it, I would be either in prison, disabled or in the graveyard.

Playing by the rules and an occasional mischief, Korhville was one of the greatest places to grow up in, nothing like growing up in the country, where neighbors were good neighbors. Fruit trees growing wild in the woods, smokehouse, vegetables, pork, and chicken.

Beef was raised by lot of the families also. That was the life, would not trade it for nothing, but there are a few things that I would do differently. Some of the guys had some nice rides back in the day and they kept them clean and running smooth. Let me see, Woody had a green 1968 Dodge Charger Rt 440, Morris had a 1959 Chevy Impala, Chubby had a 1964 Nova, James Solomon had a green 69 Mustang Fast Back with a stick shift, Freddie Williams had a 64 white Chevy Impala, Donnie had a Canary yellow 64 Chevy Impala, Boots had a 64 white Ford Galaxy, Jake (Melvin Williams) had a blue and white 72 Cutlass Supreme with oversized tires on the back and pipes sticking out the side that would burn your leg.

You had to be careful getting out of the car. Herbert had a 1957 black Chevy Bel Air; Joe Whitfield had a 1960 red Chevy Impala and Joe kept that Chevy sparkling clean. I remember one time, some of us boys went into Mr. Lonnie's watermelon patch and took some melons without his knowledge and hid them under Joe's house. A couple of days later we returned to Joe's to get the melons, but Joe had taken half the melons and given them to his relatives over in the Woods, so much for that, Ha, ha, ha. (Cypress) Shorty Stewart had a 1966 Impala, I do not know whether it was purple or blue, but I am leaning more towards purple because I keep seeing purple. Shorty kept that car clean as a whistle, most of the time when you saw Shorty or Joe, they were always wiping on their car. Buddy Whitfield had a black 1949 Ford Coupe, Koochie had a brown Ford hard top convertible that let down into the trunk and he had a Buick Deuce and a Quarter, Terry had a red and black Malibu and a 1963 green Ford Fairlane. Marion Blakes, whom we call big Blake, had a gold and brown Deuce and a Quarter. Blake was an, easy going guy with a winning smile and distinctive voice and a calmness, about him, he was and still is a winner today. (On KTSU radio 90.9 hanging out with Chatter Box in the early AM on Saturday mornings) I support and salute KTSU and its staff. Shout out to you big Blake (Marion Blakes Jr.) and Chatter Box. (Larry Hale) We appreciate what you do.

Okay, enough about some of the bad boys and cars, I want to touch a little bit on the Hanky Panky side of Korhville, but not in great details, I would have to leave the Country. (USA) When I was a young lad, during my early and late teens, I saw a lot of things going on that I should not have seen. Hanging with or around the older folks, I got to be in places that teenagers were not allowed without being in the company of an older person.

My older sister started me out, she would take me to beer joints and cafes with her so when she drove back home in the night, she would not be alone. That is how I started drinking beer, she would buy me a Soda pop and pour me a little beer in it. Her spot was Annie's and Joe Brady's, up around Tomball and Hufsmith Texas. It was there that I first heard the record by Jimmy Hughes, "Steal Away".

I never did forget that record, because the people would be hugged up slow dancing, man, I could not wait until I was old enough to get out and go on my own, hang out with the grown-ups, slow dance and such.

I remember, one time when I was riding my bicycle to the store, I noticed the guy who I was working for, (hauling hay) had his truck parked on the side of the road, (West Montgomery road) I was on the little dirt road. (Hufsmith-Korhville road) Curiosity got the better of me, so on my way back from the store, I decided to stop and look in the woods. You see, there were woods separating the two streets. Low and behold, there he was, with a strange woman. I jumped on my bike and rode off as fast as I could, but not before they spotted me. I was scared that he was going to do something bad to me for what I had seen. I wished I had never stopped.

After that I would always hide and avoid him, until one day the lady bumped into me walking to the store and she told me that he wanted to talk to me and that he was not going to hurt me or do anything to me.

I reluctantly started back working for him and we became good friends, anyway it was not my business. What I discovered though, is that he liked strange women. He parked on the side of the road on another street.

We were somewhere else one night when he did it this time, after we were done working for the day.

He left me inside the truck while he went to the back door of a house to visit another strange woman. We will just call him Jody, old Jody was a slick one, but I liked him because we had become friends and he would let me drink a beer with him.

Peyton Place and daytime Soap Operas do not have nothing on little Korhville when it comes to secrets and romance.

As I have stated, I was able to hang with older boys and men, they took me under their wings and taught me things. My father had died when I was 12 years old, I had to grow up fast.

For what it is worth, they were just people being people, doing what was good and not so good, but they kept us in line. If I wrote a book about Korhville in full, I could not do Korhville enough justice. I value friendship and family, more than money or fame. I could not tell about all that I saw, know and did. I could not tell it all because some of the old folks confided in me and told me stuff that I could not write about and other things that I saw and know that I cannot write about and would never write about, because of my love and out of a good conscious. There is not much that happened that I cannot speak on, about good times, and bad times. As the old folks would say, let it rest son. The only reason I talked about old Jody is because no one knows him but me. That's a wrap.

To my knowledge, there are only a couple of things that warranted crying about and a lot of funny things that happened during my teen and adult life while growing up in Korhville Texas. All in all, the memories are fond and there were some exciting times. Except for a couple of sneaky Petes, and old Jody, life was about normal.

There was only the one white on black incident where the young black man who was shot in the back while trying to run into the store to get out of harm's way. The white man who did the shooting was not from Korhville Texas and the young man never recovered from his injury. That was a sad situation and it still brings tears to my eyes.

Then there was a young girl who had an operation to remove cancer from a part of her body.

We used to tease her because we thought that she was just faking to get attention, an attempt at being the teacher's pet. We did not know until she went into the Hospital and had the surgery, that she had cancer. We all felt bad for teasing her about being the teacher's pet. That was a teachable moment for us, one that I have not forgotten.

Let me step away from those two stories, it brings too much sadness back to my heart. Moving on there were some funny incidents with the old and young men alike. There were these two old men that carried their rifles with them everywhere they went, reason being, they were protecting themselves from each other, one was scared and the other one was glad. I believe they both were scared, anyway, nothing never happened. They both died from natural causes at a ripe old age, but there is a story behind why they carried those rifles.

Some of the funny incidents were because of love triangles and man's drunkenness. Men leaving the beer joint on Saturday night, falling in the ditch by the graveyard, passing out and never making it home.

One man would come and get his brother out the ditch on Sunday mornings before Church started so people would not see him in the ditch like that. How do I know? Because we lived in a small house right next to the graveyard and I could see him from the kitchen window. Korhville had its moments of bad conducts and interesting ventures.

One man kicked another man's door in because he fell in love with the man's girlfriend, and again, how do I know? I was with the carpenter when he got the assignment to repair the door before anyone could know what happened.

There was an incident one day involving one of the rowdy bunch's little brother and a couple of his cohorts.

They were shooting at some of the Korhville boys running through the woods. One of the guys running ran over to this old lady named Aunt Frank. My mother was there visiting Aunt Frank and when the guy knocked on the door and told them who he was and who was chasing him, Aunt Frank told my mother not to open the door. Aunt Frank told him to go and hide in the outhouse (outdoor toilet).

That is what he did and when everything cleared, it was late that evening before the rest of the guys found him. It turned out to be a laughable moment.

Then there was the incident where one of the boys used to go in this old woman's field and steal her watermelons. She had warned him to stay out of her watermelon patch.

He did not listen, so she put a spell on him, yes, she did, the spell stayed with him for years until the woman died, straight up, no joke. He had a nervous twitch for years.

It did not and do not pay to disrespect the elderly or do them harm, in any way shape or form, I am a living witness.

There are a lot of little funny things that occurred in Korhville Texas back in the day, but it is too long a story, and

173

there are some good memories with a few bad, but the good out-weighs the bad by a long shot.

Let us talk about my age group, Jake, Perk, Butt, Yogi, Dan Bug, Woody, little Ike, Tickle Britches, Bubba, Chubby, Red, Spur, Boots and me, that is a whole book by itself, not to mention a host of other guys and girls. It would stretch from Korhville to Tomball, Hufsmith, the Grove, Cypress, (the woods) Acres Homes, Studewood, the Wards, downtown Houston, and Louisiana. I was all over the place when I was growing up, got to see a lot and do a lot. Life was good growing up in Korhville Texas with my family, good neighbors, and all my good friends. I would not have it any other way.

There was a downside to going to Louisiana in the summer during school break. My grandparents lived there, and my mother would take us for a visit every summer, we would catch a train from Houston. The downside was that when you stayed with grandpa, you had to get up early before the crack of dawn and catch that truck to the cotton field and pick some cotton. Man, that was a bummer.

Now do not get me wrong, I was not afraid of work, I began working at the age of 8, but cotton was just not my cup of tea. Plus working all day picking cotton only yielded me $1.50 cents, from 5:am in the morning until 5:pm in the evening. It was back breaking work and I was only 12 years old at the time. Wait, let me go back to working at 8 years old.

You see I was the only boy in a house full of females, my mother and 5 sisters, my other sister was staying with our grandparents in Opelousas Louisiana.

I have 6 sisters total and that left me with having to do most all the wood chopping, emptying the slop jar, cutting the grass, and packing water.

I put a broke wagon together to haul wood from out of nearby woods and hauling water from the Church and School house well. By the time I reached 12 years old I was well known as that Latin boy, and if the old folk wanted something done, they would say, get that Latin boy, he is a good, hard worker. There is one thing that the old folks did not believe in and that is, being lazy. I did odd jobs for elderly people in the community who had no children, or their children were away. I dug flower beds, chopped wood, picked berries, and harvested fruits for some, such as figs, pears, peaches, and plums. I was kept busy. even before I was 12 years old, I worked alongside my mother in the fields, pulling and shucking corn, picking peas, digging potatoes and hoeing peanuts. Sometimes the only way we ate a good meal was to help shell peas, shuck corn, churn butter, milk cows and pluck chickens at a neighbor's house.

Then there was the meat packing plant that would give away meat that they did not eat or sell to the community, such as chicken feet, hog heads, ox tails, chitlings, tripe, pig feet, liver, neckbones, and pig ears. Today it is sold in stores everywhere. My mother did wonders raising us, she only had a 3rd grade education and her heritage being Indian. Her mother was full blooded Choctaw Indian. She lost contact with her people on her mother side and we only know the people on her father's side. She raised us with a firm hand, belt, switch and whatever was in her reach. She was God fearing and taught us to be the same. The Lord provided us with good neighbors and good friends wherever we went.

Now back to me, during my younger years and part of my adult life, I walked around barefooted all the time. I only had one pair of shoes and those were my Sunday go to meetings.

I also managed to get a pair of hand me downs, PF Flyers tennis for my school shoes.

Supposedly they would make you run faster and jump higher. I went barefooted unless I was in school or going to Church, whether it was working in the fields, digging flower beds. Going into the woods to chop wood, walking in the deep hot sand, or picking berries, I did it all barefooted.

As I look back over my life in Korhville, I cry sometimes, not because of the hard or bad times, but because I look at what my mother endured raising and providing for her children and grandchildren and how I used to hear her praying for us and other families in the community. I think about how God took care of her and her children, blessing us with a God fearing, loving and caring community, from Korhville to Hufsmith, to Tomball and Acres Homes.

Everywhere my mother went, she was well received, her and her children, she was known as Sister Latin, Mable and some just called her Mrs. Latin, but the most used was Sister Latin. We were for the most part, well behaved kids, we knew the punishment for disobedience, a good whupping. No back talking, no butting in, no asking for nothing whether we were at someone's house or at the store.

That was a big, no-no and she did not spare the rod. Let me talk about today for a minute. Children complaining about what they are going to eat tomorrow or the next day and what are they going to wear. Today people throw away just about as much food as they eat, do not mention the nice clothes that are trashed because of a new fashion. We waste a lot.

I remember being ashamed to wear blue jeans with holes or patches or faded. Now they are selling at a high price. Changes, imagine that? It's all good.

I remember when there was no meat in the house, but we made do and ate what we had, bread and syrup, bread and sugar, crackers and cheese, beans and rice, rice and beans, beans and rice. There was mayo and bread, bread and butter, milk and bread, milk and cornbread, one day just corn on the cob. We survived and did not complain because we knew that our mother was doing all that she could to provide and complaining would not help, but maybe get you a scolding or good whupping.

No one starved, we also knew meat would eventually come, and we did not waste food as people do today.

Even at school the children helped each other out, for instance, if someone had a meat sandwich, they would trade it to the person with the mayo sandwich so that person would have some meat. Some traded peanut butter and jelly sandwiches for a meat sandwich. Everyone shared with those who were less fortunate. Me being poor as I was, I got a chance to give a meat sandwich for a mayo or peanut butter and jelly sandwich. It felt good being able to help someone else and it still feels good helping someone in need today.

After I say this, I am going to jump ahead, because there is just so much to tell, and I cannot tell it all. There were some exciting and great times in Korhville Texas, giving some wonderful memories and enjoying walks down country road and memory lane. Remembering Aunt Bea's little café, where soda pop, cookies, chips, candy, pickles, and the best hamburger in town was made, man, that was a good burger.

I do not want to forget, before Aunt Bea's, there was Mrs. Susie Autry, she supplied our little school with lunch. She would bring from home, her baked and fried goods at lunch time and sell to the children and teachers. She cooked a mean blackberry cobbler and the fried chicken was on point. Then there was Reverend Green who sold big red plums during summer vocational Bible school for a nickel a cup, and if you did not have a nickel, he would give you a cup anyway. That is the type of people who lived and shaped the community of Korhville Texas.

Mr. Ike passing by our house every Sunday morning going to ring the church bell and he also rang the bell when someone died, that is how the word got around. Mrs. Jane going collect the mail at the box on the corner of Hufsmith-Korhville and Spring Cypress, then delivering the mail to the people in the community. Mrs. Loy cooking homemade bread and fruit pies, filling the air with the sweet aroma of some good old home cooking. Yeah buddy.

I used to love going over to her house to play with Tee and Chubby, her two boys.

She would always let us lick the cake bowl and give us a small pie to taste when they were ready. Shirley, Mrs. Lottie, and Mrs. Creasy making homemade preserves and giving us the leftovers from the peaches, plums, figs, and pears after they had cut off what they needed for baking or preserving.

Watching the men make homemade sausage and sometimes helping them by taking turns turning the crank on the meat grinder, then hanging the meat in the smokehouse.

Sometimes on weekends at gatherings we would make homemade ice cream. The older folks would have us young boys take turns turning the crank on the ice cream maker.

Having Christmas programs at the Church and school, then receiving small brown bags of goodies. The bag consisted of an orange, apple, assorted nuts, candy and if you were lucky you may get a bag with 2 oranges and an apple or 2 apples and an orange, the nuts and candy. We celebrated the 19th of June every year. We enjoyed the good Bar B que Preacher, Marie and Oscar would cook for the whole community, free of charge and Preacher supplied everything. Gone are those days.

Working after school, on weekends and during the summer, mostly hauling hay. Most of us worked for Preacher, he had a lot of hay trucks and a Sanitation route. I also worked hauling hay for others, such as Mr. George Stewart, Mr. Nathan Woods, Gus, and Biggie.

Mr. George used to tell us some wild stories about growing up in his day, and about some things that went on back then.

Every so often the older folks would allow a house party at one of their homes, but under strict supervision. We enjoyed hayrides, picnics and trips to Galveston beach.

I am so grateful for the older men who took me under their wings, looked out for me and taught me the value of a dollar, work ethics and how to be respectful.

Elder Charles E. Solomon, Mr. Junior Solomon, Mr. Boy Solomon, Mr. O'Neal Woods, Mr. Ren, Mr. Square, Mr. George, Mr. Nathan, Preacher, Mr. Tena Amos, Uncle Ira,

Walter Cossey and Mack. I worked for Mack 10 years doing body work on cars. I cannot leave out Uncle Ike Cossey, Mr. A.J. Cossey, big papa Arthur Cossey, and Archie Cossey.

I still have the Bible Reverend Archie gave me when I got shot the first time, during the middle seventies.

Mr. Junior would stop by and pick me up so that I could ride with him and James so I would have a father figure to attend the banquets they had at Klein High School for the FFA class because his son James and I were in that class together.

Elder Charles E. Solomon was my Pastor and Bible teacher

during that time, and he kept me in line and mindful of doing the right thing and to obey my mother. I had a lot of help from the men of Korhville while I was growing up.

Mr. Tee Hubbard would hire me to do little odd jobs for him, like cleaning out his attic, stacking wood and cleaning his Bar B que shack. I always kept some sort of job.

Having money to spend at the small grocery stores was a blessing and it felt good having your own money to spend.

Cookies were 2 for a penny, soda was a nickel to a dime, Ice cream was a nickel to 35 cents, depending on what you bought. We bought marbles, spinning tops, yoyos, cap pistols, and slingshots, but the slingshots also had another name. that I cannot use. (derogatory)

It was not always peaches and cream for me, because I had to fight my way to be excepted by the guys in my age group.

The number one culprit was Perk, James Blanton at the time, which after the dust settled, we became the best of friends and die-hard brothers.

Perk was not the only one, Melvin, Wilbert, Joe Cossey, Chubby, then there was Dan Bug, my cousin, Willie B. Hardy, Freddie Stewart and Lonnie Jr. (Plank) Herbert, Jerry, and Marvin Jeffery. (Dino)

I did not win every fight, but I won the ones that mattered, such as beating Perk and Dan Bug. Tee made me beat Dan Bug, he told me that if I did not beat Dan Bug, that I was going to have to fight him. (Tee) That did it.

Perk was a hard fight, because we fought more than once, until I became established as a fighter and not a scary cat or pushover. Joe and Wilbert were the strongest of all the guys in the bunch, but I was faster with my maneuvers. Joe and I got into a fight on the bus one evening after school.

We were fighting close to the back door of the bus and when Joe swung at me, I ducked, causing him to miss and he ended up knocking the back window out of the bus.

Now, you can believe that was the last fight we had, because I did not want to get hit by Joe. Wilbert on the other hand, I used a wrestling move on him, and he gave up, for some

reason Tee was always around, except for the fight on the bus.
Well, it was official, I was one of the boys, a full blooded Korhvillian with A-1 approval. Oh yeah, just so you know, I did fight B.J, but it was only one punch thrown. I hit him with a sucker punch when he was looking down and then I ran away. He went crying to the principal and I got a whupping for that and that was the end of it.
There was the time when I worked with Cecil Barnes, Bubba Richard and Terry Taylor training racehorses over on Boudreaux road off Hufsmith-Korhville road. It was fun until we started getting the bad ones, wild horses that walked on you when they bucked you off. I was the first to quit, that was not my cup of tea. I should have quit when I saw a horse throw one of the fellows and walked all in his chest and the boss man looked at me laughingly and asked if I wanted to try to ride him. No sir, not I. He was not paying us enough anyway.
I quit 3 jobs in my teenage years, all because they worked you like a slave and paid next to nothing, it was 4 jobs, the 4th was with a group. A group of us boys from Korhville quit a job because the man did not want to feed us, and he only gave us $6.50 cent for a day's work. It was back breaking work, so we quit in the middle of the stream. We started walking home but was picked up by white friends from Klein high school.
The first job I quit was working at a dairy, herding in the milk cows, feeding the cows, cleaning the facility and stacking hay. At the end of the week the man left me hanging, he and his family had gone somewhere without paying me and when Monday came, I went to get paid and he gives me a $15.00 check. That was it for me, I quit.
Then working with the racehorses was really some back breaking work, having to clean each stall, feed and water the horses, groom them and not to mention the riding, getting
bucked off and bruised. After my first week I received a check for, here we go again, $15.00, amazing, I guess I had $15.00 written on my forehead. I could not cash the check

anywhere that weekend. I gave it back to him that Monday for cash money and walked away.

I grant you, this was in the early and mid-60s, and $15'00 must have been the thing for some back then, because when we were hauling hay for Preacher, that is what he paid us teenagers. $3.00 a day, $15.00 a week. Of course, you could buy a lot for $15.00 back then.

For the $3.00 a day, we youngsters were supposed to just sit in the truck and steer or guide it through the hay field, between the rows and bales of hay, while the men or older boys tossed the hay onto the truck and stacked it. Most of the time, the older guys would make us younger guys, (drivers) get out and throw the hay onto the truck and they would do the driving. They took our easy job.

Complaining to the boss fell on deaf ears because the guys doing it were his brothers. Eventually, as we got older and jobs became more plentiful, we got raises, thanks to the competition. Just touching on some of the things Korhville had, being a small community and black settlement. We had most of what we needed. We had the love, the caring, faith leaders, good neighbors, Churches, a school, farmers and peddlers. We had levees and creeks to swim in and smokehouses for the cured meats.

We had a canteen and burger café, beer joints, fruit trees, vegetable farms, cattle, horses, chickens, pigs, turkeys, wild game, country stores, horses and wagons, cars, trucks and God fearing, people. I am changing gears now, let me move to a different scene here.

I remember when we young guys used to hate passing by Woody's house because he would always make his dog chase us and grab us by our pants leg.

We would try to sneak by, but Woody was always on the lookout for us, peeping out the window, waiting on a victim. He would run out the house and then call that old dog, Sam.

Although he had 4 dogs, Sam, Tick, Red and Hotshot. Sam being the youngest, is the only one that he would make chase us. Sam would grab you by your pants leg and be pulling on you, growling, tearing your pants and sometimes biting you, but not bad enough to be concerned about going to a doctor or needing medical treatment.

One day when I was passing by, he made Sam chase me and I ran into the woods and climbed up a tree, thinking I was safe, but Woody started throwing sticks at me to make me come down. I reluctantly came down and the dog grabbed my pants and Woody was happy that his dog had treed me and grabbed me by my pants. Yeah, but one day, my chance came for revenge when we were over to Aunt Susie's. We were putting some cows in the corral, low and behold, I saw a yellow jacket nest in the corner of the barn, right above Woody's head. Okay, now there was an idea taking form.

What do you think I did? Yes, I did, I picked up some dirt, threw and hit that nest and the yellow jackets stung Woody all upside the head, he was running, hitting at them and hollering. He wanted to beat me up, but Tee and Aunt Susie would not let him, plus I lied, told them I did not see the nest, and that I was throwing at one of the cows. Woody was hotter than a branding iron.

There was one thing about growing up in the country, Korhville, and that is, that whenever we had a fight or misunderstanding, we shook it off and we were back friends the next day or that same day.

There were no drive-bys, killings, or holding grudges, we held no ill will towards one another, also, we got a whupping for fighting if your parents found out about it.

As I look back and see where the Lord has brought me from, the good and the bad times, I always see the good times outweighing the bad times. God is good.

Life for me as a teenager, for the most part was grand, because growing up without a father as a teenager was not a piece of cake, but with the Lord on my side, watching over me with a God fearing mother, I made it, Glory be to God.

The Lord blessed me to encounter good people, friends and neighbors who took me under their wings. I had more mothers than anyone could hope for, women like, Mrs. Lottie, the mid-wife, Mrs. Janie Pearl, Aunt Sarah and Mrs. Jane, Mrs. Verdell, Mrs. Mildred, Mrs. Myrtle, Mrs. Lessie

Mae, three Mrs. Annies,- (2 Solomons and 1 Williams) Mrs. Yetti Mae, Mrs. Loy, Aunt Bea, Mrs. Julia, Mrs. Creasy and Mrs. Lillian, Aunt Nellie Curtis, Mrs. Thelma, Aunt Frank, Aunt Sofi, Sister Eddie Lee Hardy, Mrs. Alberta, Missionary Stewart, Sister Alice, Mrs. Emma, Aunt Susie, Mrs. Gist, Mrs. Caroline and of course, my mother Mrs. Mable Latin. I was chastised by them all, whether it was verbally or physically. I know I probably missed a few, you know at 70 years old, every now and then, my memory will wonder away or try to hide from me and get lost in the shuffle.

If I could tell it all, you would see that I really did have a wonderful life growing up in the country, between Korhville, Tomball and Hufsmith. (less the self-made trouble)

What a lot of my Korhvillians do not know and some just may not remember, is that I lived in Tomball and Hufsmith Texas, just up the road, a hoot and holler away.

In Hufsmith we lived with my daddy in the summer when school was out and his house was down by the Taylors, where he used to farm corn and watermelons. I remember one of the Taylors, Jaybird, my daddy used to take me over to his house to get a haircut. Jaybird's wife used to cut my hair. She would put a bowl on top of my head and cut around it and leave me with little bangs, sometimes we called them pompadour. Jaybird used to tease me about it and laugh, whenever he saw me. Jaybird was a real cool guy with a great personality, a great sense of humor and a great family.

One day my sisters and I asked our daddy if we could go out in the garden and pick some corn, he said yes, but what we did not know at the time, is that he was drunk. We went out and picked 4 sacks of green corn, we did not know anything about whether the corn was ripe or not.

We went out in the field and just started pulling corn, filling up the sacks, thinking that we were doing good. We each had picked a full sack of corn.

Well, when our daddy woke up and saw those sacks of green corn, he gave us all a whupping, saying he did not tell us to pick any corn. That is when we discovered his drunk side.

There was one more incident with our daddy before we decided not to go and stay with him anymore. He went to the store to get a loaf of bread and when he came back, he was drunk and empty handed. I went down the road a little ways and there it was, he had fallen and dropped the loaf of bread in the ditch, I picked it up, ran home and that was the last time we stayed with our daddy, (pa) as we called him. Then we stayed on Snook's lane, in Tomball, you could throw a small rock from Tomball to Hufsmith, that is how close they are, and no pun intended.

There were great people in both places, and we were blessed with great friends wherever we planted our feet. The Matthews, Doakes, Lees, Richards, Wilsons, Taylors, Holidays, Johnsons, Bradys, Turks, Chaneys, Barnes, Blackshears, Simmons, Spurlocks, Wootens, Allens, Browns, Vicks, Lots, a different family of Curtis, Weatherbys, McGee, Norris, Washingtons, Maids, Hogans, Osbornes, Sadlers, Martins, Wares, Polks, Porters, Humphreys, McPhersons, Montgomerys, and the Godfreys.

Sam, Henry, Milton, Donald, Bubba and I used to play marbles, trade comic books and walk to the store in Hufsmith, and buy our supply of marbles and spinning tops. We were all good marble shooters, but I think Henry was the best one of all us, he shot good and he had a good aim.

I used to go over to one friend's house on Saturdays to watch westerns, like the Lone ranger, cowboys and Indians.

We would lay down on the dirt floor in front of the tv, while his mother would be cleaning and cooking.

Although I had made a lot of friends on Snook's Lane, my first year at school in Hufsmith was not so easy. You see, I had a bully who had his eyes on my lunch. Yes, he took my lunch a few times, I know, I hate to admit it, but it happened. I was not always the guy people know today and me in my late teen years, no sir, I had not yet established my fighting skills and toughness to make a stand and back it up. That was yet to come, it was still in the developing stage, I was a green horn, with no skills. Remember, I had no father figure in my life at that time, just a bunch of females.

I credit Archie, Chester Allen's brother with helping me to stop forking over my lunch to the bully. Archie was the custodian at the school and he saw what was going on one day, so he gave me a free ice cream sandwich and told me that I needed to stand up for myself and stop letting that fellow take my sandwich. Thanks to Archie, for those encouraging words, he was so kind.

Well I made my stand, yes, I was scared, but it was now or never time and I did it, no more giving up my lunch and we became good friends and are still friends to this day. That happened back in the early sixties (61-63) We never fought physically; I just drew the line and made my stand.

After I got acquainted with the guys and became well known, I gained friends like Leon, Danny Boy, Clarence, Milton, (Booga) Lee, Ray, James, Leroy, Sam and Henry, Donald, Bubba, Henry and George Vick, Richard Don, Lee Arthur, Ira Don, Willie Magee, Spurlock, Jo Joe and Sam, Donald Joe and Howard. Then there were Wayne, John and Jessie, Willie Rogers, Joe Boy. Sonny Boy, Toe Joe, Willie Plue, I guess I better quit while I am ahead, my memory getting foggy.

I was just trying to touch on some of the places and people in my life doing my teen years, it's just so much to tell, I would need to write a novel or two, part one and part two.

Oh yeah, I almost forgot about my old friend, Mr. Buddy Roxie, we used to go by and visit with Mr. Buddy and he would always call me, LyeLou, instead of Elijah, I do not know why, he just did, for his own reason I guess. Yep, good old Mr. Buddy, he was a good old fellow.

Thanks for the memories, Tomball, Hufsmith and Korhville, you were great and still shines for me, I salute you and country living. Stay prayed up and prosper.

Now back to Korhville for some final words, I need to mention that after Aunt Bea's good burgers, came Molly's smoked slice beef sandwich and burgers, I can vouch for the slice beef, it was good, others swear on the burgers, but I loved the slice beef sandwich, besides, that was much later in my life.

Let me get back on track with my teen years, of making mischief and the sowing of my young wild oats.

Here are some of the little things or small trouble that I got into that only warranted a whupping and not jailing.

I used to go and hide in the graveyard at night, right before Church let out and I would put on a white sheet and make ghostly noises to scare my nieces as they passed by with their grandma, my mother. They would be hollering and running, but my mother would say, "that isn't nobody but that old boy" then she would call my name, "Nook, Nook, come out of there and stop scaring these children," I would be laughing and come out. Those were fun times.

One time at school, while in the top of a tree, where we all would gather and play, I decided to make it rain in the top of a fellow's head and I got two whippings for that little stunt, by the Principal and my mother.

Then there was the incident involving another tree at the edge of the woods where we had tied a rope on a limb so that we could use the rope to swing over the ditch of water. It was working fine, we all would take turns swinging back and forth across the water, until I got the bright idea of loosening the rope so the next person swinging across would fall into the water. I climbed up to where the rope was tied around the limb and when I was asked what I was doing, I told them that I was tying the rope tighter.

The next person in line was Art, (Arthur Lee) as soon as he got halfway across the water, the rope came loose, and he fell into the water and got all wet.

Imagine that, I was accused of untying the rope, anyway we all had a good laugh and it was at recess, so Art had to go to class the rest of the day with wet pants.

There was the time when we went camping and that first night after we had set up camp, we went exploring in the woods.

We came upon Mr. Ren's mule. Now I had some help this time, my cousin and myself, we scared that mule and it ran off into the dark night and fell into the gully. That old mule

let out a loud bellow when it hit the bottom, the gully was dry.
Then there was the time when I would put a stick in the middle of the dirt road down by the graveyard and watch drivers as they went in the ditch almost, just to get around it.
Mr. A.J. Cossey came along, stopped and examined it, then moved the stick out of the road, spoiled my little fun.
I am going to write about a few more incidents and then I will be done telling on myself.
Morris, Darlene, Charlotte, Karen and I were playing in the sand at the edge of the road in front of Mrs. Lottie's. I threw some sand in Darlene's face, I did not think anyone had seen me, until Mrs. Lottie hollered, "come here boy, I saw you." Darlene was jumping around and crying.
Mrs. Lottie made me come in the house, kneel down in front of a storage chest at the foot of her bed, while folding a rope into four ropes, meaning when she hit me I would be receiving four licks at one time, very clever.
Let me tell you how this went down, she only got a chance to hit me them four licks one time, because after that first hit, I jumped up and ran out that room, passed Hattie Pearl, Darlene's mother, who was typing and laughing, as I ran by, with Mrs. Lottie in hot pursuit, yelling," come back here," no way, I was out of there. I ran all the way home.
I did not escape for long, once Mrs. Lottie told my mother what I had did, I got another whupping, yep, that is right, two whippings for the same incident.
Then there were the times when Perk, B.J., Jake, Butt, and I would go out to the barn where Mr. Ike hid his whiskey. We would take us a sip, just enough to not be noticed, but I think he knew because he would tell us to stay out of the barn, do not play in the barn.
Now this one is about the time that we listened to my cousin and got ourselves into trouble.
We were standing on the corner of Hufsmith Korhville road and West Montgomery Road, selling berries.
There were Jerry 1 and Jerry 2, but it was Jerry 1 that was with us that day. Bub, Morris and me, we had about 2 gallons

of berries left between us and we had about 7-8 empty buckets.

My cousin came up with the idea of us putting dirt in the bottom of the empty buckets to stretch our berries out to make more gallons. It was getting late in the evening and if somebody stopped for berries, we could let them take the buckets with them. So, here we go, we filled some of the empty buckets halfway with dirt and poured some berries on top of the dirt, making the bucket look like it was full of berries.

We managed to make about 5-6 gallons of berries out of 2 gallons. A white man stopped to buy the berries, but he did not have any containers to put the berries in, so we boys being nice, we told him that he could take the buckets and that we had plenty buckets at home and that there was no charge.

The man was happy, we were happy, everybody was happy, he even tipped us, we tried to refuse it, but he insisted.

Well, it was only a matter of time, it was unescapable, we all knew that the man would be back, the question was, when?

When came the very next evening, we were on the corner with 7 gallons of berries. Let me describe this favorite corner spot of ours if I may. It was a culvert there that had a small cement wall about two to two and a half feet tall, about 6-8 inches wide and about 6-8 feet long. We could sit all our berries on it, and we could even sit down.

I was the first to see the man coming, I was on guard because I knew he was coming back. No one believed me until it was too late to run. Man, I saw that old green truck a mile away.

The man run up on us, jumped out the truck, flashed some old badge at us, which did not frighten us, but we knew that we were wrong for what we had did.

The man told us about how happy his wife was when he showed her all those gallons of berries that he had bought her and that she had mentioned how big and pretty they were and then when she dumped them in the sink, all that dirt came out the buckets into the sink.

We ended up giving the man all our berries that evening, six or seven gallons, give or take one.

Had we not given them up he probably was prepared to take them anyway, since he was flashing his little badge, but you can bet he brought containers to put the berries in that time.

At least it all ended well, and we did not try that anymore, and that is what we got for listening to Dan Bug, my cousin, the troublemaker. He was known for throwing rocks and hiding his hand and laughing at you. So much for that.

I remember when our mother used to spray for mosquitos at night. She would come in the room where we were sleeping and start spraying over our heads. You had to hurry and cover up or you would get spray in your face, then she would say, just cover your head and keep spraying. Mosquitos and bedbugs were bad back then.

She believed in that spray gun. Before I forget there was an incident where some white people tried to rope me and two of my sisters as we walked from the corner store. It was a man and woman. The woman was driving, and the man was on the back of the truck twirling a rope. When they got close to us, he tried to lasso one of us but failed, so we ran into the woods. They tried to lure us out with some soda pop. They set a couple of bottles out on the side of the road.

The soda was open and foaming like something had been put in it. We were smarter than that.

We watched all this from the safety of the woods from behind some brush and trees. We decided it was best to run all the way home through the woods. When we reached the house our white neighbor, Mr. Turner was passing by and we were hollering and telling our mother what had happened. Mr. Turner heard us, so he went down the road to confront the people, but they were gone. That was a very scary moment for us but thank the Lord that we had sense enough not to fall for their little trickery.

Now you know a little something about my teen years, growing up in Korhville Texas and neighboring towns.

I thank the Lord every day for his Grace and Mercy, for watching over me when I was young and foolish and in my adult life, for all he has down for me and my family, friends, and neighbors.

Wait a minute, I must tell you about the incident with old Koochie, (Horace) before I go.

Me, my cousin, and a couple of the fellows were headed up in the Prairie by Lump's mother's house to go swimming in the rice field levee. Dan Bug got me in trouble again. We stopped by Mr. George Stewart's house to get a drink of water and we saw Koochie fast asleep in a chair and Dan Bug had the bright idea for me to put a piece of paper between Koochie's toes and set it on fire. I set the paper afire, when it burned down to Koochie's toes he let out a loud scream and his mother came to see what was going on. Koochie had jumped up and was trying to catch me, all the time my cousin was laughing. Mrs. Mildred, Koochie's mother whupped me and we left there and went on to the swimming hole with me a little sadder. So much for my mischief adventures.

Before closing, I would like to mention some of the girls that I grew up with during my teen years.

Dorothy B., Geraldine, Dorothy Green, Annie W., Jean W., Linda W., Lola A., Gwen, Maxine, Katherine S., Brenda Faye, Helen, Annie, Linda S. Gwen, Linda, Ann, Erlene, Connie, Trina, Faye, Cathy, Carol, Katherine, Nancy, Erma, Elizabeth, Margaret, Georgia, Julia, Nissie, Bren and Rose, Dorothy C., Delores, Margret and Sharon, Margaret Ann, Caroline, Cheryl, Debra, and Jackie, Karen, Minnie Lee, Midget, Margaret S. Ethyl, Ruby, Betty, Verna Mae, Debra Green, Hattie Pearl, Gladys, Betty and Bobby H., Mollie J., Lillian J., Lela Kaye, Fucial, Tasa, Johnnie S,(peaches), Caroline S., Sandra S., Donna M.C, Juanita, Rose J., and Cynthia Curtis.

My sisters, Joyce, Barb, Helen, Vollie May, Dot and Rose.

Lucy, Joanie, Patricia, Carla, Lola, Denise, Rose, Juanita, Rosie, Mary, Brenda, Darlene, Eva, Sharron, Darlene, and, Charlotte, Joann, Claire Nell, Mary-Lou (sister Carter). Dorothy Blanton, Dorothy Green and Little Annie Woods were running buddies, when you saw one, you saw the other.

I must also mention, Mrs. Irene, Mrs. Billie S., Mrs. Shirley and Emma, Sister Ella Thomas, Sister Eddie Lee, although they are my seniors, I could not leave them out.

Their homes, my family did visit a lot and they knew me when I was a teenager. I ate at their tables, and they helped raised and chasten me.

As I continue to look back over my life growing up in the country, in Korhville Texas, I cannot help but think about how we all were good neighbors to one another.

How we came together in a time of crisis or need and helped each other to survive. We withstood the worst of times and the storms that came our way. We survived hurricanes, flooding and hard times together. We had more than two hurricanes but the two that I remember clearly are hurricane Carla in the year and summer of 1961.

I was 11 years old, and hurricane Beulah in 1967, I was 17 years old and they both happened in the months of September. They were the worst ones that I remember while growing up in Korhville, besides that, I have a niece named after Carla, and she is mean just like the hurricane. I am just kidding, I better clean that up, we do not want to stir up the hurricane.

I remember after hurricane Carla, Mr. Isiah Carter sent me to the store to get him some unfiltered camel cigarettes and some two for a penny, cookies. I waded in water almost knee deep all the way to the store and on the way back, I do not know how I did it, but I dropped the bag with the cookies in the water and got some of them wet.

After that it all went downhill, I started eating some of the dry cookies and thinking of a story that I could tell to justify the cookies being wet and crumbled.

An idea came to me to tell Mr. Ziah that a truck came by and splashed water up on me and I had the bag in my hand, so the cookies got wet, yeah that was it.

I went with that story, it sounded good to me, so I kind of dragged my feet getting back. When I finally arrived, Mr. Ziah was sitting on his porch as usual and he did not look happy to see me. I wonder why?

I reluctantly handed him the cigarettes and wet bag of cookies, and he almost cursed me, he said, what is this? How the cookies get wet and these are not all the cookies I sent after, where is the rest of my cookies, boy?

I told him my made-up story and he told me to stop lying and gave the bag of wet cookies back to me and said, "you eat them, that is all you are getting.

He said, I was going to give you a nickel, now I am not giving you nothing. I will not be sending you to the store anymore."

He was hotter than a pepper pudding, he opened the pack of smokes and examined them to see if any of them were wet.

He found a couple wet ones and I heard him cursing under his breath as I was leaving the yard.

That did not go over too well, but of course Mr. Ziah, that is what everybody called Mr. Isiah. Well, Mr. Ziah eventually got over his anger and started back sending me to the store, but said, do not get nothing wet now, you hear. I was not a real bad kid, neither were any of the other kids in Korhville, we were just boys and girls being country kids. We pop fireworks on the 4th of July, we celebrated the 19th of June, we went to Church and Sunday school. We did chores after school and we had innocent house parties and we respected our elderly and all women and girls.

There was always a grown up that you feared more than anybody else and for me and most of us it was Mrs. Lottie, Mrs. Creasy and sister Julia Woods.

Mrs. Lottie could outrun you, if you ran from her, she could catch you, Mrs. Creasy would pull your ears and sister Julia did not play. We were told that sister Julia could roll out on her belly and shoot you with her shot gun and think nothing of it. I think they were just pulling our leg.

Sister Julia was kind of mean but sweet in her own way, if you did not cross her you were alright. My mother was friends with her and whenever we walked down that hot dusty, thick sanded road to visit her, we would end up either shelling peas or churning butter.

One thing about sister Julia, she made good use of her company, and so did a lot of other people that we visited.

That was their way, while you had company, put them to work, let them help you with your chores while shooting the breeze, I guess you can say that was a good concept and cheap labor.

Do not get me wrong, I am not complaining, because sometimes that is the only way we ate, by being over at someone else house and helping them with whatever they were doing, so at lunch or supper time they would feed us.

So we all profited from the visits. The people whose homes were opened to us most frequently were the Cosseys, especially Mr. Walter and his wife Mrs. Thelma. My mother and Mrs. Thelma would be in the kitchen shelling peas while we children were outside playing, but every now and then we had a hand in shelling peas or other chores.

As I look back, I can see my mother and Mrs. Thelma through that kitchen window talking and laughing as they shelled peas.

The other Cosseys were Mr. Ike and Aunt Sarah, we ate many meals at their table also. We were either shucking corn or digging potatoes because there was always something to do.

There were 5 sets of Solomons, and we ate at all their homes as well, Mr. M. senior, Mr. M. junior, Mr. Charles E., Mr. Willis Solomon, (Mr. Boy) and Mrs. Wilora Solomon.

Now do not get upset families, because this is just my opinion, Mrs. Loy had the best food, reason being, she cooked them homemade pies, biscuits and bread and would give me and the boys, Tee and Larry (Chubby) a pie apiece whenever she was cooking and I was over there playing with the boys.

Look, man you could smell that bread and pies cooking just passing by on the road, just imagine being in the yard. When we were playing, we would play close by the back door because that is where the kitchen was, close to the back of the house.

I think she knew this because she would be smiling when she looked out the window or hollered out the window and told us to stop playing so rough before someone got hurt. Then much to our surprise she would walk to the back door and call us and give us each a small handmade apple or peach pie. You cannot argue with that. I want to mention these people because they were pioneers and good neighbors in Korhville, and to shorten the story, I am going to bunch the rest together.

There were the Greens, Lonnie Green and his wife, Mr. Joe Williams and his wife Mrs. Annie and the Woods, Mr. O'Neal, and his wife Mrs. Willie Bea.(Aunt Bea)

The Hardys, sister Eddie Lee and Otto Powell, the Stewarts, Mr. George and Mrs. Mildred, Mr. Ezekiel and Mrs. Myrtle and of course uncle, Ira and Aunt Nellie.

Mr. Square Williams and Mrs. Lottie supplied us with the yard bird, because they had chickens running around free. Open range chickens and if they wondered over to our house, they were fair game, okayed by both parties mentioned.

Then there was Aunt Frank, Mrs. Wortham who we spent a many nights and days at her home helping her out, because she had no children that I know of. We fed the chickens, cows, pigs and helped make homemade sausage. She had a small smokehouse out behind her house.

Uncle Ira and Aunt Nellie had moved to Korhville before us.

All the families mentioned are families who supported us and let us share meals with them at their tables. When I look back or talk about Korhville I cannot help but to remember those men and women who have gone on and left a legacy of friendship, value, love and caring one for another to live on forever in a place that they settled in and called home. They paved the way for children, grandchildren and great grandchildren to make their mark.

They shall never be forgotten; their memories live on. Amen. I hope you enjoyed my little walk down memory lane, giving insight into my life growing up in the country, Korhville Texas, I sort of got a little carried away, caught up in the moment, so to speak. I did not mean to write this much, but it is all good.

My hat is off to the pioneer men and women of Korhville Texas who sacrificed and laid down a solid foundation for their children, my family and future generations of

Korhvillians. The children and community of Korhville still work together as their ancestors did in keeping and preserving the heritage of the black settlement of Korhville Texas.

Some of the descendants of the pioneers who keeps records, preserves and keep the cemetery from going unrecognized or unkept are men and women like, Mrs. Irene Mosely, Katherine Stewart, JoAnn Williams, Freddie Williams, Richard Green, Melvin Williams, James Solomon and all the others who works hard towards that goal.

Question?

When was the last time you had some homemade butter, biscuits, flap jacks, homemade sausage from the smokehouse, milk straight from the cow, homemade ice cream, some good old Brer rabbit syrup or tasty homemade preserves, a chicken picked straight off the yard, fried or smothered in gravy, good old buttermilk, fruits picked fresh from the tree, berries right off the vine, homemade pies fresh from the oven, and homemade crackling and good old chicken and dumplings?

Yummy, yum, yum! Yeah, I hear you, me too.

Old school and most of the country folk knows exactly what I am talking about. One thing though, milk straight from the cow today may not be a good idea, too much stuff floating around nowadays, from chemicals to diseases, so be safe with whatever you do and pray over all your food before you eat it.

Again, I hope you enjoyed the short story of part of my early life and time in Korhville Texas as a teenager growing up during segregation and integration, I caught the last of the Jim crow. We could not drink here, could not go there, could not sit here, could not eat there, go to the back, colored only, white only etc. I need to mention this, there was this one place that we used to go to eat, a white café where we had to go to the back to eat. Well, that was fine for us because the women cooking, we knew and grew up with. We ate just as good in the back as the people eating out front. The women, which were young girls then, would load our plates up with whatever we ordered. We could not help but leave satisfied. Even after integration and we were able to eat in the front, we still went to the back because we were served a greater helping of food and the service was better in the back.

Thank you, young ladies of Hufsmith Texas, we really appreciated you during a time of difficult years, making our visits and meals very enjoyable.

Now even though the place has moved up on the main highway and is bigger and better, I have not been inside of it yet. Maybe one day soon, I'm looking forward to it.

Korhville Texas

It was a small settlement between Houston and Tomball,
I always enjoyed the Spring and the Fall.
There were large families like the Stewarts and Cosseys,
Korhville had no lawmen or Posse.

Most of the Stewarts lived North, out on the prairie plain,
On Hufsmith-Korhville road and Ezekiel lane.
They had horses, cows, chickens and a few fruit trees,
Even had an old barn full of honeybees.

There were the Williams, the Fergusons and the Woods,
With neighbors, families shared their goods,
There were some Greens, Williams and Cosseys who farmed,
There was no need to be armed.

The Solomons were a large family with hearts of gold,
They would not leave you out in the cold.
If a man took sick, neighbors would come and lend a hand,
They would even help to work his land.

There were the Amos, Curtis, Latins, Whitfields and Carters.
In Korhville, we swam in muddy waters.
There were Roundtrees, Blackshears, Autrys and Lees,

Some of the Williams and Solomons had plum trees.

The Hardys were another large family with caring hearts,
In building up Korhville, they all had parts.
Most of the meat was dressed and stored in a smokehouse,
Traps were set for the mouse.

Every family man in Korhville worked for a living,
They were not slack in sharing and giving.
In Korhville Texas the Lord was good to us all,
On weekends we had a ball.

Let us continue in peace, prosperity, good will and love,
Knowing that our help comes from above.
Some mothers and prayer warriors have died and gone,
Now the children must carry on.

It is time for us all to stand up and be bold,
The Word of Truth must be told.
Without the power of prayer, we shall be at a great lost,
Our souls will pay the cost.

The time has come to stop partying and having fun,
From all evil we must run
Friends and neighbors withstood many storms together,
They fellowshipped in good and bad weather.

Hearing that old rooster flap his wings and crow,
Watching the lovely wildflowers grow.
The kids had to be home before the sun went down.
Our big thrill was going to town.

My Favorite Eating Places

Burn's Original BBQ (Acres Homes best*****)
8307 De Priest St,
Acres Homes, Texas 77088 (the **44**) "Hello Burns"
H-Town (Houston, Tx)
Burns also has burgers on the spot. "Way to go Burns!"
Now I have a little nephew, **William Lee** (Still Bill)
He knows his way around the pit too, he grills some
mean **Pork Neck Bones,** Chicken/Ribs, no contest.

Gatlin's BBQ (*****)
3510 Ella Blvd
H-Town (Houston, Tx) 77018
Gatlin's has a nice atmosphere and their customer service is great. (A-1) Keep doing your thing Gatlin.
Note: Gatlin's also serves breakfast, 7am-10am, enjoy

Seafood

Verna Mae's Po'boys Seafood &More
(1st choice*****)
16010 West Rd
Houston, Texas 77095
(Verna Mae's recommended to me by Edith Blackshear)
(aka-Lottie Black)

My Soul Food Places

Farmer's Fresh Meat (*****)
(1st choice, good food with great/friendly service)
They also serve breakfast (7:00 am-10:00 am)
9541 Mesa Dr.
Houston, Texas 77078

Turkey Leg Hut (*****)
4830 Almeda Rd
Houston, Texas 77084

My Church Home

Carverdale Community Fellowship Church Of God In Christ
[Pastor Freddie L. Solomon]
Our Church Motto:
"Impacting Lives With The Word Of God"
10028 Algiers Rd
Houston, Texas 77041
Raised in:
Solomon Temple Church of God In Christ
Pastors (were)
Charles E. Solomon (founder) **1st**
Elder H.M Bolden **2nd**
Supt. Eddie Toppen Jr. **3rd**
Honorable mentioned, Elder Burah Gatlin Jr.

Poems inspired by Pastor Freddie L. Solomon
June 21st, 2020 (father's day)

Who Is Your Daddy?

Is he one who loves the Lord, loves your mother and his children? Not a striker or abuser of authority and curser of his mother and father. Does he respect his elders?
Who is your Daddy?
Does he teach you right from wrong and guide you in the way that you should go? Is he a chaser of women and club hopper seeking entertainment? Does he respect women?
Who is your Daddy?
Is he the one who provide food for the table, put clothes on your back, provides water when you thirst and puts shoes on your feet? Is he a gambler, liar, braggart or a cheater?
Who is your Daddy?
Is he one who comforts you in a time of trouble and shelters you during the storm? Does he hang out among the wine bibbers? Is he a drunkard and womanizer?
Who is your Daddy?
Does he teach you about God and the Commandments of life and how to live as a Christian following God's laws? Is he Paying the bills, and a good role model? Does he honor his mother and father, and is he a God fearing, humble man?
Who is your Daddy?

Stop, Look Up, And Live

When you are driving your car and reach intersections, and there is a red light, flashing yellow light, a stop sign, or yield sign, look both ways, be safe and check all directions.
Stop, look up, and live.
Before you make that big step, watch where you are planting your feet, the devil is busy and supplying the world with all kinds of evil and deceit.
Stop, look up, and live.
When you are on the verge of giving up, thinking that you don't have nowhere to turn, no one to talk with, Jesus is there, don't just sit idle and let your soul burn.
Stop, look up, and live.
Don't be one who complains and accuses others when you are struggling, times get hard, and you can't see clearly, whatever you do, never accuse the Lord.
Stop, look up, and live.
Because of your hardened heart, closed ears and your blind eyes, you look for help from the bottle and cards, know that help cometh from above the skies.
Stop, look up, and live.
The Lord is your strength, the Lord is the supplier of your needs, the Lord gives life and rest, the Lord answers prayer, and you can't beat the Lord giving nor in deeds.
Stop, look up, and live, Amen. (July 12th, 2020)

"GOD IS GOOD ALL THE TIME"

A Very Special Thanks

I would like to give an incredibly special shout out and thanks to my family, friends, neighbors and to all my wonderful Facebook friends who wished me a Happy Birthday and Anniversary. Thank you all, your responses were awesome. From our hearts to yours, Please accept our humble and sincere thanks. Take care friends, be safe and may you be blessed and prosper in all that you do. We wish you nothing but the best. Amen. Elijah/Debra Latin
Thanks again for your friendship and support.